SALE'S BRIGADE

IN

AFGHANISTAN.

SALE'S BRIGADE

IN

AFGHANISTAN

WITH AN ACCOUNT OF THE

SIESURE AND DEFENCE
OF JELLALABAD

BY REV. G. H. GLEIG

CHAPLAIN-GENERAL TO THE FORCES;
AUTHOR OF 'THE SUBALTERN;' 'THE STORY OF THE BATTLE OF WATERLOO;'
'LIFE OF LORD CLIVE;' 'LIFE OF SIR THOMAS MUNRO;' ETC.

The Naval & Military Press Ltd

published in association with

FIREPOWER
The Royal Artillery Museum
Woolwich

Published by
The Naval & Military Press Ltd
Unit 10 Ridgewood Industrial Park,
Uckfield, East Sussex,
TN22 5QE England
Tel: +44 (0) 1825 749494
Fax: +44 (0) 1825 765701
www.naval-military-press.com

in association with

FIREPOWER
The Royal Artillery Museum, Woolwich
www.firepower.org.uk

The Naval & Military
Press

MILITARY HISTORY AT YOUR
FINGERTIPS

... a unique and expanding series of reference works

Working in collaboration with the foremost
regiments and institutions, as well as acknowledged
experts in their field, N&MP have assembled a
formidable array of titles including technologically
advanced CD-ROMs and facsimile reprints of
impossible-to-find rarities.

ADVERTISEMENT.

An accidental meeting with the 13th regiment at the sea-bathing quarter of Walmer during the autumn of last year gave me an opportunity of hearing more of the particulars of the Jellalabad siege than had previously been communicated to me. The narrative was full of interest when detailed by actors in the scenes which they described; and this it was which led to the determination on my part to place it permanently upon record: for brilliant as have been the exploits of many corps and brigades, as well in the Afghan as in other wars, none seems to me to have exhibited more soldier-like qualities than that which, under the late gallant and lamented Sale, fought its way from Cabul to Jellalabad, and held the latter place against a nation. The 13th Queen's and 35th Bengal Native Infantry, with the detachments of artillery, sappers, and cavalry, which co-operated with them, have won a name for bravery, endurance, and steady discipline which any regiments in any service may envy. Let me add the expression of an earnest hope, that being thus conspicuous they will take care in other and not less important respects to set an example, wherever they go, to their comrades, as well European as Asiatic.

The substance of the following story is gathered chiefly from the manuscript journals of officers engaged in the campaign.

I have consulted, likewise, the Orderly Books of the 13th, which verify every statement advanced; and the conversation of various individuals, particularly of Captain Wood, Brigade-Major at Chatham, has been of infinite use to me. One ground of deep regret there is, indeed, for me, as well as for the country at large, namely, that the noble old soldier who taught his followers thus to fight and thus to conquer, no longer survives either to approve or censure my narrative. But Sir Robert Sale died, as he himself always wished to do, on the field of battle; and his fame survives him.

G. R. G.

Chelsea, June, 1846.

(vii)

CONTENTS.

SALE'S BRIGADE

IN

AFGHANISTAN.

CHAPTER I.

Afghanistan—Its Geographical Position, Climate, and Productions.

It is impossible to fix, with any degree of accuracy, the present limits of the kingdom of Cabul. When visited by Mr. Elphinstone in 1809, it was said to extend from the west of Heraut in longitude 62°, to the eastern portion of Cashmere in longitude 77° E.; and from the mouth of the Indus in latitude 24° to the Oxus in latitude 37° N. It comprehended, according to the nomenclature of our best works, the districts of Afghanistan and Segistan, with part of Khorassan and of Makran; Balk with Tokerstan and Kelan; Cuttore, Cabul, Sindey, and Cashmere, together with a portion of Lahore and the greater part of Moultan. But besides that, even in 1809, the obedience paid to the king by many of these provinces was rather nominal than real, the subsequent progress of events has materially crippled his power, and contracted his dominions. When we speak, therefore, of the Doorannee empire as being bounded on the north by the Hindoo Cush, or Indian Caucasus, on the east by Hindostan, by the Arabian sea on the south, and by Persia on the west, we must be understood as assigning to it rather the limits by which in theory it is circumscribed, than the extent of territory throughout the whole of which the authority of the nominal government is recognised.

The population of the country thus marked out has been taken

B

at numbers varying from fifteen to nine millions. Probably the latter will be found to come, under existing circumstances, as near to the truth as the former. It is composed of many different races, of which the principal are Afghans, Belochees, Tartars of all descriptions, Persians, including Tanjiks, Indians, such as Cashmerians, Juts, &c.; besides miscellaneous tribes, which are neither numerically considerable, nor exercise any great moral or political influence in society.

The face of the country is very much diversified, being intersected in all directions by mountain ranges, which increase in altitude as you descend from the shores of the Arabian sea and the great plain of the Indus, till you reach the foot of that branch of the Himalayahs, to which the name of the Hindoo Cush has been given. The principal of these are the Khyberry hills, which follow the course of the Indus on both sides as far down as Korrabaugh, or Callabaugh, in latitude 38° S.; the Suliman mountains, which lie mainly to the west of this river, and push out numerous spurs, till they connect themselves with the mountains of Kund; the table-land, or rugged highlands of Kelaut; the Khojak mountains; the Gaùdava mountains; the Bolan; the hills about Ghuznee; and, finally, the steep ridges which overhang the elevated plain of Cabul on every side, and gradually lose themselves towards the north and east in the great Indian Caucasus.

A country thus ribbed, and of which the elevation is everywhere considerable, cannot but be, upon the whole, barren and unproductive. A large proportion of its surface is mere rock; and the pasturage in the mountainous districts, though excellent here and there, is generally scanty. Nevertheless, the valleys which pass to and fro among the hills are remarkable for the fertility of their soil, producing in abundance almost all the herbs and fruits which thrive both in Asia and in Europe: for the climate of Afghanistan (it may be best to use this term as generic of the whole) differs greatly for the better from that of Hindostan; the heat in summer being generally less intense, and the cold in winter more severe. Indeed, the snow, which never melts upon the summits of many hills besides the Hindoo Cush, comes down in smart showers upon the plains in the season, and the ice on stagnant waters is often of such a consistency as to sustain both men and horses, as in the north of Europe.

The waters of Afghanistan are the Indus—with its innumerable tributaries,—the rivers of Cabul, Kauskur and Helmund, the Urghundaub, the Khashrooa, the Ochus, a lake near Cabul, and canals and watercourses innumerable, which have been cut among the hills in different districts for purposes of irrigation. Its animal productions are as varied as the varieties perceptible in its soil. In addition to the wild beasts which thrive among ourselves, there are to be found here lions, tigers, panthers, hyænas, wolves, and bears. Both the lions and the tigers appear to be inferior in point of size and ferocity to those of Africa, and the plains of the Ganges; but they do considerable damage at times to the flocks and herds, and are occasionally, though not often, destructive to human life. One breed of horses—that reared in the district of Heraut— is excellent ; the rest are for the most part yaboos or ponies, but they are exceedingly hardy and sure of foot, and, as well as camels and asses, are numerous. There is no lack of cattle, and sheep and goats are abundant. We find here, also, dogs, some of which, especially the greyhounds, would be highly prized in Leicestershire; hawks, trained and untrained ; for falconry is a favourite sport with the Afghan chiefs ; and, as to domestic poultry, every species which you meet in England is to be met with here. Insects and reptiles likewise abound ; but of the latter few are dangerous, for all of the serpent kind appear to be harmless ; and the bite of the centipede and scorpion, though it may trouble for a while, has never been known to prove fatal. Finally, the herbage, wherever it finds soil on which to grow, is to the eye of a European peculiarly attractive, while most of the trees, shrubs, flowers, fruits, grain, and grasses which come to perfection in the temperate regions thrive here, with many which require the suns of a tropical climate to mature and bring them to perfection.

The state of society in Afghanistan is now, and seems from time immemorial to have been, entirely different from that which prevails in other countries of Asia. In name the government is monarchical ; but the authority of the monarch, except in the great towns and throughout the districts immediately dependent upon them, extends no farther over his subjects than the authority of the first Jameses extended in Scotland over the clans which occupied the most inaccessible of the highland districts.   Indeed, the Afghans bear, in this respect, a striking resemblance to the Celtic portions of the population both of Scotland and of Ireland, that they are divided into tribes, clans, and septs, which pay little or no obedience, in the internal management of their affairs, to any power except that of custom and of their chiefs.   To be sure, there is a point in which the spirit of clanship in Afghanistan acts differently, and on principle too, from its manner of operation either in Scotland or in Ireland. In the latter countries the head of the tribe used to demand and obtain the fealty of his clansmen to his person; in the former this fealty is paid more to the community than to the chief: and hence it comes to pass that there is much more of individual independence of character among the Afghans than seems to have prevailed among the ancestors of the MacNeils or the O'Connors; for though there are instances in the history of the Celtic clans of the setting aside by his people of one chief and the appointment on the same authority of another, the proceeding was not only rare in itself, but seems never to have been resorted to except in the last emergency; whereas in Afghanistan the practice is of constant occurrence as often as by the representatives of the principal families the chief is held to be incompetent; or is found guilty of having transgressed those unwritten laws which are understood by all, and by all reverenced and obeyed from one generation to another.

The principal tribes among the Afghans are four, which branch off respectively into a countless number of clans.   These are the Doorannees, the Ghilzies or Ghiljies, the Khyberrees, and the Beelooches, of which the Doorannees have, for the last hundred years, possessed a preponderating political influence, though the Ghilzies are perhaps numerically the stronger, and, as individuals, assert the utmost conceivable share of personal independence. The latter, indeed, are noted, even among the wild tribes of the Caucasus, for their ferocity.   Portions of them, which inhabit the regions between Cabul and Jellalabad, have doubtless been reduced, by the weight of the crown, to a certain show of order; but the clans which dwell in the districts that extend from Candahar to Ghuznee are described as removed by a very slight bar from savageism.   Two of these, the Oktaks and the Tohkees, are said by one who sojourned a good while among them, to be, as regards their male population, " unsurpassed by any other Afghan tribe for commanding stature and strength ;" but it cannot be added that they use these advantages well, for " their manners are brutal," and the violence of their chiefs, in their intercourse with strangers, is often such " that they can scarcely be considered in the light of human beings." Neither can much be stated in praise of their gentleness, whatever other good quality may be possessed by the Khyberree septs. They rob all merchants, travellers, and strangers whom they can way-lay, and practise perpetual forays on the lands of their neigh-bours ; but they never murder in cold blood. An individual may be slain in the attempt to defend his property ; a whole kaffela or caravan may be cut to pieces ; but such an event as a deli-berate assassination, except for the furtherance of a political end, seems to be unknown among them. Like their Celtic proto-types they are, moreover, hospitable in the extreme, and as ready to give a cloak to one wayfaring man who may need it, as to take a cloak away from another whom they may attack. If you throw yourself upon them in their own homes, you may almost always assure yourself of protection ; but it does not by any means follow that, having escorted you to the extreme limits of their territory, and seen you fairly across the line, they shall not fall upon you the next minute and plunder you of every article of value that you possess.

Except in such clans as these, which may be reckoned among the Caucasian Children of the Mist, the Afghans appear to be a sociable and even a romantic people. The intercourse between the sexes is, with them, on a far better footing than with other tribes which profess the faith of Moslem. Indeed, the Afghan's home deserves to be accounted such, for he shares his hours of leisure pleasantly with his wife and children ; and if a guest (not a European) arrive at his dwelling, he leads him, without scruple, into the circle. The consequence is, that the passion of love, as we understand the term, is neither unknown nor un-honoured in Afghanistan. It enters into the subject of almost all the songs and tales which pass current in the country, and exer-cises no trivial influence at times over the transactions of real life. A love passage between the chieftain of one clan and the wife of the chief of another, led to a long and fierce war between the houses, in the course of which, as both clans had numerous allies, much blood was shed. It is a remarkable fact also, that some of the most illustrious warriors and princes of this nation have been as much celebrated for their skill in poetry as in arms. Khutal Khan, the chief of the tribe of the Khuttucks, whose resistance to Arungzebe might stand a comparison with that of Sir William Wallace to Edward the First, was the most popular poet of his day, and struck his lyre with excellent effect as often as it was found necessary to reanimate the spirits of his countrymen when depressed by defeat. His songs and odes continue to be in great favour throughout Afghanistan to this day.

Few of the Oriental nations have any high regard for truth, or consider that they are bound by promises, however solemnly uttered. The Afghans can hardly be said to form an exception to this rule; yet the best authorities represent them as at least knowing what truth is; and adhering to it, except when the advancement of some scheme of paramount importance in their own eyes seems to require its violation. In other respects also they differ widely from their neighbours on either hand of them. There is no indolence or effeminacy in their natural dispositions: on the contrary, they are hardy, enduring, patient of fatigue, and, when occupied in any business or employment that interests them, industrious to a remarkable extent. As horsemen they equal the Tartars, or the Indian dwellers upon the Pampas of South America. Slavery prevails among them, but in a very modified and irrepulsive form. To a man they are fond of money: nevertheless they do not hesitate to scatter it freely round them, provided they have reason to expect that, by so doing, they will secure the accomplishment of some important or much-desired end. They are proud, and jealous of neglect by their superiors. A clansman will attend cheerfully in the hall of his chief, as the chief waits upon the sovereign, from day to day; and so long as the superior continues to treat the inferior with courtesy, it is well. But let this be interrupted, even so far as that the salutation of the latter is not returned, and, without making a display of his mortification, the inferior forthwith absents himself. In a word, the Afghans, like other portions of the great human family, have their virtues as well as their vices, both modified, if not produced, by the point in civilization to which they have attained. Their vices are revenge, cruelty, avarice, rapacity, jealousy, and a paltering on great occasions with good faith. Their virtues, love of liberty, fidelity to friends, kindness to dependants, hospitality, bravery, hardihood, frugality, patience of labour, and prudence.

The mass of the people who inhabit the towns do not belong to either of the four great Afghan tribes. They are the descendants of the various races which have at different times broken in upon Afghanistan and established there a temporary supremacy, and who are now, and for some generations past have been, reduced to a state of vassalage. Indeed, it is in Afghanistan somewhat as it used to be in England ere the Norman and Saxon races amalgamated, that the feebler, though more numerous portion of the community, carry on its ordinary business and practise trades, while they who exercise dominion over the land dwell apart chiefly in their country-houses. The court is indeed Afghan; so is the army; and the Afghan courtiers and commanders of troops occupy mansions in the capital as long as attendance on the sovereign is required. But the shopkeepers and tradesmen in Cabul are almost all Taujeeks, while banking is conducted exclusively by Hindoos. It is not, however, meant that among merchants on a large scale Afghans are never to be found. Commerce they do not consider as degrading: it is trade alone which they despise; though, generally speaking, the chiefs seek employment about the court, from which they withdraw at stated seasons to their castles, that they may superintend the gathering in of their harvests and indulge in the pleasures of the chase, to which they are much addicted.

Of the Afghan tribes some are agricultural, others pastoral. The agricultural clans possess settled habitations; the pastoral hordes dwell in tents; which they remove from place to place as the desire of obtaining better forage for their flocks and herds may prompt. Five distinct orders of persons find employment and a subsistence in agriculture. These are, first, such owners of the soil as cultivate their own lands, employing for that purpose hired labourers; next, tenants who occupy farms at a fixed rent, either in money or in kind; thirdly, middle-men, or land-

stewards, who, applying a stipulated portion of the produce
to their own use, manage the whole estate for the owner.
Fourthly, there are hired labourers—freemen—who, for nine
months in the year, engage to serve either a tenant or a land-
owner, and are remunerated, sometimes by a mixed payment of
money, food, and clothing; sometimes by money-wages alone.
If the latter arrangement be effected, the labourer receives for
his term of service about thirty rupees: if the former, his re-
ceipts fluctuate between two maunds and a half of grain with
one rupee, and ten maunds with two rupees. Lastly, there are
serfs (*adscripti glœbœ*) which go with the land, however frequently it may change its owners.

Labourers are hired in the towns by the day, and receive for
their day's work from fourpence half-penny to sevenpence of
our money,—enormous wages in a country where from five to ten
pounds of the best wheaten flour are sold for twopence; for
wheaten bread constitutes in Afghanistan the ordinary food of
the people, though rice, and occasionally Indian corn, is consumed; while the horses are fed with barley, the cattle during
the winter with turnips, and both cattle and horses, when the
occasion requires, with carrots.

From what root the Afghans are sprung it is not an easy
matter to determine. The Taujeeks, of whom mention has just
been made, are of a mixed Arab and Persian descent, being the
children of the hordes which first introduced Mohammedanism
into the country, and, driving the aborigines to the hills, kept
almost exclusive possession of the plains during three centuries: but the origin of each of the four great tribes is lost
in obscurity. They themselves have a tradition that they are
the descendants of the ten tribes whom Shalmanezer carried
away captive after the destruction of Samaria; and the account
which they give of that catastrophe is both curious and striking.
Indeed, they go further than this; for they claim kindred with a
royal stock, asserting that they are sprung from Ismia or Reskia,
one of the sons of Saul. Unfortunately, however, for this tradition, the name of Reskia or Ismia, as a son of Saul, does not
occur in the Bible; and in other respects their genealogies
savour very much of the fabulous. Besides, their language bears
no very close affinity either to the Hebrew or the ancient Chaldee.

Out of two hundred and eight words, which Mr. Elphinstone took the trouble to compare with Persian, Zend, Pehlevee, Sanscrit, Hindostanee, Arabic, Armenian, Georgian, Hebrew, and Chaldee, one hundred and ten were found to be radically different from all. The rest could be traced back to one or other of the six former dialects; whereas with the four latter they proved to have no connexion. The Afghan seems therefore to be an original language, in the strictest sense of the term; and is stated by those who are acquainted with it to be rough, but expressive and manly. The people themselves call it Pushtoo, though the character of which they make use is the Persian. A curious theory is entertained respecting this matter by one whose judgment it is right to treat with respect. Mr. Masson considers the Pushtoo to be a version of the Pali, that ancient language of which traces are to be found well nigh all over the world; which was spoken by the Phœnicians, the people of Carthage, of Tyre, and even of Italy; and which the Hyksos, or shepherd-kings, brought with them from the East into Egypt; and continued as the Philistines to make use of down to the days of the descendants of David, and long afterwards.

The best authorities agree in describing the Afghans, especially in their towns, as a sociable and lively people. They delight in evening parties, where their principal amusement is story-telling. They have their concerts likewise, and nautches, of which the latter are said to be in a great measure free from the indelicate movements which characterise those of Hindostan. They are great people for pleasure parties into the country, and play marbles up to grey hairs with extreme relish. Their more athletic sports are firing at marks, hawking, riding down partridges, and battue-shooting; and they are much excited by witnessing the combats of quails, cocks, dogs, rams, and even camels.

There are other peculiarities in the domestic manners of the Afghans which deserve to be especially noticed. To the nature of the chiefship in each of the principal tribes allusion has already been made; as, for example, that the office is hereditary, and that the power, though controlled by recognised and established usages, is very considerable. This hereditary right, however, implies no more than that the chief, or Khan, for the

time being, shall derive his descent from one of the leading
families of the sept; for it is the king who confers the dignity;
and though an abandonment of this principle is sure to give
offence, and sometimes leads to civil war, there are many instances on record of a stranger being placed over the whole
community, though seldom to a good purpose. At the same
time the chief, after he is nominated and has been accepted by the
tribe, can in himself perform no act of sovereignty, but must
consult with his Jeerga; that is, a council of elders, consisting of the heads of the principal families in the tribe. To be
sure, if a sudden emergency occur, or some matter of trivial
moment demand a settlement, the khan or chief is permitted to
act alone; but an attempt to render himself independent of the
Jeerga, where time and opportunity of calling it together might
be afforded, would inevitably lead to mischief, and end either in
the deposition of the khan, or the severance from the tribe of
such septs as might feel that they were strong enough to set up
for themselves.

Feuds and quarrels of long standing appear to exist among
the tribes of Central Asia to as great an extent as they formerly
prevailed in the Highlands of Scotland. To this, indeed, the
universal recognition of the *lex talionis* leads; for where individuals assert the right to avenge their own wrongs, and vindicate
their own honour, there can be no escape from the ascendancy
of the fiercer passions, which are never assuaged in a day.
Moreover, he who touches the honour or attacks the rights of
any one member of a clan, touches the honour or attacks the
rights of all; and a family war once begun, continues to be
waged often throughout three or more generations. Then
follow forays and wasting of lands with fire and sword, which
there is no power in the supreme government to suppress; for, in
point of fact, the supreme government is never appealed to except
in the last extremity.

The law of Afghanistan is, in theory, the same with that of
Mohammedan countries in general—that of the Khoran. In
practice the people manage their affairs and adjust the differences
according to Pushtoonwullie, or immemorial usage. This it is
which adjudges an eye to be given for an eye, and a tooth for a
tooth; and enables the party wronged to avenge himself on a

relative, if circumstances prevent him from reaching the aggressor in person. Hence revenge becomes, among the Afghans, a point of honour which no man may waive except with disgrace, though he may nurse and hide the sentiment for many years, till a fit opportunity of making a display of it occur. At the same time it is fair to add, that if quarrels arise within a clan, the clan uses every endeavour to adjust them without bloodshed. Sometimes the chief is privileged to interfere, though only as a mediator or adviser. Sometimes the council of elders takes the matter up, and compels a reconciliation, on pain of expulsion: or, lastly, the khan, or head of the tribe, may be appealed to ; when he not only forces the offending party to make restitution, but levies upon him a fine for the benefit of the state.

In all these respects, the parallel between the state of society in Central Asia, and among the Celtic nations of Europe five centuries ago, is very striking. There are other points in which the Afghans appear to resemble the Germans, as Tacitus has described them. An Afghan tribe never refuses the rights of hospitality to a suppliant. He who flies from his clan, even if stained with blood, is sheltered or protected by the sept, on whose mercy he throws himself, war itself being preferred to the disgrace of rendering up a client. Again, when any great public event is at issue—if the honour or interests of the nation seem to be in danger—if foreign war be meditated, or the means of defence against invasion from abroad demand attention, the khans, or heads of tribes, assemble, and deliberate in public council on the measures which it may be most expedient to pursue. Having determined upon these, they assign to the shah, or king, authority to carry them into execution ; and obey, or are expected to obey, his bequests implicitly as long as the danger lasts. But the occasion ended, things return to their former course, for the monarchy has little or nothing of the temper of an autocracy about it. Indeed that kingdom is a mere amalgamation of many independent republics ; the king, the mere head of this confederation,—whose influence is felt in the capital and in other great towns where he may chance to have governors, but who exercises little or no authority over the dwellers in the glens and among mountains. The service which his chiefs render to him is merely feudal. He may arrange for tribute instead of soldiers, and impose taxes on the traders and merchants who dwell around the palace; but this tribute he seldom gets in, except with the strong hand, and neither in the amount nor manner of collecting his taxes does he seem to be guided by any fixed rule.

Finally, a king of Cabul is not only such, but he is khan or chief of the most warlike and powerful of the Afghan tribes. And in this particular also, his position bears a remarkable resemblance to that of the kings of Scotland, while as yet the royal house of Stuart occupied the throne in the northern division of Great Britain.

CHAPTER II.

Outline of Afghan History.

THERE was a time, some centuries ago, when the Doorannee empire, in respect to its power and extent, held a high place among the nations of the earth. The Afghans have repeatedly given sovereigns both to Persia and to Hindostan ; and with both countries their wars, aggressive and defensive, have been endless. It was among them, also, as numerous coins and other relics attest, that the Macedonian colonies of Alexandria ad Caucasum, of Arigæum, and Bazera were established ; indeed, there is a tribe inhabiting the mountain districts north of Lughman and Khonar, whose complexion, hair, features, and general appearance seem to vouch for the descent which they claim from the wreck of Alexander's army. But Afghanistan could not, any more than the countries that border upon it, sustain the attacks of the enthusiastic propagators of the faith of Mohammed, and yielded, for a while, reluctant obedience to the rule of the Caliphs. Other revolutions followed. As their conquerors sank into effeminacy and indolence the mountaineers recovered their courage, and, headed by kings of the Ghilzie tribe, not only threw off the Persian yoke, but became lords of Persia itself. Then arose Nadir Shah, before whose strong right hand all opposition went down. The Persian crown was wrested from its Afghan wearer ; the Persian arms were once more dominant in Afghanistan ; and Delhi itself felt the weight of a sceptre which was wielded to crush rather than to protect. Nevertheless, among these hardy mountaineers the spirit of independence was not extinguished. They found a new leader in Ahmed Khan, a principal man in the Suddozye family, one of the most powerful of the clans into which the tribe of Abdallees, otherwise Doorannees, was divided ; and by him they were conducted through a series of great exploits and marvellous successes, not only to independence, but to a wide extension of their empire.

Ahmed Shah was a prudent politician as well as a great and

successful warrior. He innovated in no alarming degree upon
the usages of his country ; yet attached to himself and to his
government the nobles and heads of houses, by finding for them
constant employment and much gain in military operations.
His object was rather to extend than to consolidate the empire ;
and he attained it. The whole of the Punjaub and of Sinde
were tributary to him. Twice he marched to Delhi, and four
times to different points within the Indian empire. In the west
he carried his arms as far as Neshapoor and Astrabad. It was
he who changed the style of his tribe from Abdallee to Doorannee, having himself assumed, at his coronation, the title of
Dooree Dooran; that is, the pearl of the age. He died, worn
out by constant exertion of body and mind, in the fiftieth year
of his age ; and left the monarchy which he had founded to his
eldest son, Timour.

Timour Shah possessed no portion of the enterprise, and very
little of the talent and vigour of mind, which distinguished his
father. He wished to reign in sloth, preferring the pomp to the
reality of kingship, and for twenty years kept his seat without
the actual loss of any of the provinces. But in his day the seed
was sown which advanced to rapid maturity under his successors ;
for the children of Timour were numerous, and fought for the
succession, and amid the confusion incident to these civil wars
the sovereignty passed from the whole of them.

Five, out of the many sons of Timour, played conspicuous
parts in this ruinous game: namely, Humayoon, the eldest by
one wife ; Shah Zemaun and Shah Shujah, by another ; Shah
Mahmoud and Prince Ferooz Oodeen, by a third. Of these,
Shah Zemaun—the succession not having been fixed,—proclaimed
himself king on his father's decease in 1793 ; and through the
influence of Poynder Khan, otherwise Serafrauz Khan, chief of
the powerful Doorannee tribe of Baurickzye, and with the help
of other lords, he secured the city of Cabul. He forthwith sent
an army against Candahar, of which his brother Humayoon
was in possession ; and of which the inhabitants seemed disposed,
at first, to support the elder branch. But Humayoon did not
possess the vigour of character which belonged to Shah Zemaun.
His troops fought badly : he was defeated, and became a fugitive ; and before the end of the year fell into his brother's hands,
and was blinded.

While these struggles went on, Mahmoud, who had acknow-ledged Zemaun's authority, was permitted to retain his position as Hakim, or governor, at Herat.   Prince Ferooz Oodeen also was with him, and seemed disposed, at first, to remain quiet ; but by and bye some differences between them arose, whereupon the prince made a pilgrimage to Mecca, and on his return fixed his residence at Iram.   Of him history henceforth makes mention as Hadjee Ferooz.

Shah Zemaun was popular, and might have kept the empire, and transmitted it to his descendants, had he given himself to the task of consolidating its looser parts ; but this wise policy he neglected, and, entrusting the management of affairs at home to a vizeer who abused his confidence, he wasted his resources in constant, though fruitless invasions of India.   His absence called into activity the ambition of his brother Mahmoud, which long lay dormant ; and on three separate occasions, in 1794, 1797, and 1799, he raised the standard of rebellion.   But he invariably sustained defeat ; and was driven at length to take refuge at the court of Persia, where he was flattered or neglected according as suited best the peculiar views which happened at the moment to be in favour with the government of Tehran.

Meanwhile the vizeer, Wuffadar Khan, had rendered both him-self and his master so obnoxious to the nobles that a plot was entered into for putting the minister to death, for deposing Shah Zemaun, and setting up his brother by the same mother, Shah Shujah.   At the head of this conspiracy, six of the principal chiefs of the Doorannee and Kuzylebash tribes placed themselves. And so well, for a time, were matters managed, that though they held frequent meetings at each other's houses, no suspicion of any evil design seems to have been entertained.   Unfortu-nately for themselves, however, they had admitted a moonshee, or scribe, into their confidence, who betrayed them, and put the vizeer on his guard.   Three individuals, namely, Serafrauz Khan, chief of the Baurackzyes ; Mohammed Azeem Khan, chief of the Alleckozyes ; and Ameer Arslan Khan, head of the powerful Persian tribe of Jewansheer, were stated to be the ringleaders ; and one by one they were seized.   Mohammed Azeem, consi-dered the most formidable of the whole, gave himself up without resistance.   An officer was then sent to apprehend Serafrauz

Khan, whose son, Futteh Khan, proposed to put the functionary to death; but Serafrauz refused to follow that daring course, and submitted. A like fate befel Ameer Arslan, who happened at the time to be resident about court; and the whole, with their partners in the conspiracy, and two other suspected chiefs besides, were summarily executed.

Great and general was the indignation excited among the members of the Doorannee tribe, and one of them, Futteh Khan, the same who counselled resistance to the order of arrest, meditated revenge. He found out Mahmoud, who, with a slender retinue, was passing from place to place in Khorassan. He urged him to withdraw from his Persian allies, and to throw himself unreservedly among his kindred; and Mahmoud, listening to the suggestion, entered the country of the Doorannee tribe, with only fifty horsemen in his train. To a man the clansmen declared in his favour; and after some fighting, and a great deal of treachery on all hands, Zemaun, attended by his late vizeer, Wuffadar, became a fugitive. They halted to refresh at the castle of one Moollah Aushik, a chieftain of the Shianwarree clan, and a dependant or protégé of the vizeer. This man betrayed them; and Wuffadar and his brothers being put to death upon the spot, Zemaun was blinded and carried to Cabul, in the Balla Hissaur, or citadel, of which he became a state prisoner.

Mahmoud ascended the throne amid the triumphant shouts of his adherents, but was soon found not to possess any of the qualities which are necessary to command the respect of a turbulent people. He regarded nothing but his own pleasures, leaving both the cares of government and the toils of war to his ministers. These were able men, for Futteh Khan was one of them; but they either did not dare, or proved little inclined to interfere with the humours of their brother chiefs; and the whole country became in consequence one wide field of private quarrel and military licence. Moreover, though the capital and the districts dependent upon it acknowledged Mahmoud, the provinces paid no heed to his behests. His brother Ferooz, while he rendered to him a nominal allegiance, seized and held Heraut. The north-eastern countries would acknowledge no other sovereign than Zemaun; and suddenly a new rival sprang up in the person of Prince Shujah-ool-Mulk, the full brother of Zemaun Khan, and a young man about twenty years of age. This youth, who had been left in Peshawur with a small party of Zemaun's guards, to take care of his family and jewels, no sooner recovered from the panic which the first tidings of the revolution occasioned, than he came to the resolution of proclaiming himself king ; and by a liberal distribution of money among the tribes in the neighbourhood soon saw the greater part of them gather round his standard.

To march upon Cabul with ten thousand men was his obvious policy, and he adopted it; but being met by Futteh Khan at the head of three thousand, in a narrow plain bounded by hills, he was totally defeated. He escaped with difficulty to the settlements of the Khyberees, by whom he was sheltered. Meanwhile a more serious rebellion, if such it deserve to be called, had broken out in another quarter, and the constitution of the empire was shaken to its foundation. The next most powerful tribe to the Doorannees was that of the Ghilzies, who in ancient days used to give a king to the whole of the Afghan nation, and who, having faithfully preserved their genealogies, set up Abdooreheem as the living representative of the old royal family. Some bloody battles were fought between the rival factions, which ended in favour of the Doorannees, though not till the fortunes of the victors had more than once been reduced to the lowest ebb, and Shujah-ool-Mulk having sustained a second defeat, the throne of Mahmoud seemed to be secure. But it was not so. Persia had taken advantage of the civil war to complete the conquest of a large portion of Khorassan. The head of the Beloches refused to acknowledge so feeble a government : of the Afghan tribes themselves, many set up for independence ; and the treasury being empty, and the king altogether wanting in personal weight and influence, there were no means at hand whereby to reduce them to order. Under these circumstances Futteh Khan was directed to march with as strong a force as could be collected against the factions. He levied a fine upon Peshawur, extorted fifty thousand rupees from the chief of Cashmere, and passing through different districts, raised the revenue from each, and came, in the summer of 1803, to Candahar. But while he thus exerted himself, the death of his colleague Akram Khan in Cabul precipitated the downfal of Mahmoud. Released from the restraint which his ministers used to put upon him, the dis-

c

solute king ran into all manner of excesses, and being eagerly
copied by his Kuzylebash guards, the whole city became con-
vulsed with rapine and licentiousness. There were chiefs there,
particularly one Mookhtar Oodowlah, who could not endure the
degradation to which the nation seemed to be reduced; and
these provoking a sort of religious revolt, destroyed the king's
guards, and shut him up in the Bala Hissaur. They then sent
for Shujah-ool-Mulk, whom they proclaimed; and having met
and defeated Futteh Khan, when marching to the relief of
Mahmoud, they compelled the latter to surrender himself, and
placed Shujah on the throne.

Shah Shujah-ool-Mulk ascended the throne of Cabul in 1803.
If deficient in energy, and therefore little qualified to fill the
arduous station to which he had been raised, the accounts of his
very enemies agree in representing him as placable, humane,
generous, and, as far as circumstances would allow, just and
true to his word. The difficulties, indeed, which beset him, and
led to his eventual overthrow, had their roots in these dispositions; for he treated Mahmoud tenderly, sparing his eye-
sight—and made no endeavour to escape from the many engagements into which, while playing an up-hill game, he had entered.
The consequences were, that the revenue was all expended in a
vain endeavour to appease the cupidity of men who proved to be
insatiable, and that the troops, kept far in arrear with their pay,
ceased to be trustworthy. Of these circumstances the partisans
of Mahmoud made good use. Futteh Khan, in particular,
smarting under the mortification to which he had been subjected,
by the rejection of his proposal, to become vizier under the new
régime, went into rebellion, and after a succession of conspiracies
and revolts—which it would be as tedious as unprofitable to
particularise—Shujah was again driven into exile, whereupon
Mahmoud, his brother, resumed the reins of government.

These events befel in 1809, a season of some anxiety to the
British government, when Napoleon was understood to be nego-
ciating with Russia and Persia for the free passage of his troops,
if not for assistance, in the invasion of India. The deposed
Shah fled for safety into the Punjaub, where Runjeet Singh was
now supreme; but the Afghan empire did not, in consequence,
obtain rest. On the contrary, there was war in all its borders;

chief after chief asserting his independence, and Persia, the ancient enemy of the whole, pressing them continually. Of Shah Shujah's repeated attempts to recover the throne, between 1809 and 1815, the space at our command will not permit us to take particular notice. Enough is done, when we state, that though gallantly undertaken, they all failed mainly through some constitutional weakness on the part of the Shah, which rendered him incapable of directing the movements of an army in the field ; so that he became the object during their progress, of much treacherous treatment, as well from his own chiefs as from Runjeet Singh. From these he finally delivered himself by escaping with his family across the English frontier ; within which, at the town of Loodianah, an honourable asylum was afforded him.

While Shujah-ool-Mulk thus dwelt in safety under the protection of the British standard, there had arisen between Shah Mahmoud and his powerful vizeer, Futteh Khan, grounds of mutual altercation, which led, in due time, to very tragical results. The brothers of the vizeer, be it observed, were everywhere established in places of influence and power. One executed the office of Governor of Cabul ; another was supreme at Peshawur ; a third was at the head of affairs in Cashmere— in a word, the strength of the empire was in their hands. Heraut, however, was held by Hajee Ferooz Deen, the brother of Shah Mahmoud, to whose son the Shah had given his daughter in marriage ; and the Shah, having become jealous of his relative, desired to gain possession of the place. Futteh Khan heartily co-operated with him, though, as was alleged, for selfish purposes, and a plan was arranged for getting the Hajee, who suspected no evil, into the power of his brother.

It had long been the policy of Persia to open a way for her armies into the heart of Central Asia ; and to gain Heraut, and establish there a base for future operations, was a measure often attempted, though heretofore without success. Hajee Ferooz Deen complained that he was threatened with a siege, and Futteh Khan, putting himself at the head of the royal army, marched to his relief. There followed in his train the youngest of his brothers, Dost Mohammed by name ; a young man who on many previous occasions had given proof of extreme courage and a

c 2

very reckless disposition ; and to him the vizeer committed the
task of accomplishing by guile that which the application of
mere force would have probably failed to effect.   The Afghans
met the Persians, and a battle ensued, from which each party
withdrew, under the impression that it had sustained a defeat : nevertheless the vizeer rallied his forces under the walls
of Heraut ; and a series of intrigues began, with the results of
which we are, for the present, alone concerned.   The unsus-
pecting Hajee was persuaded to visit the vizeer at his camp, and
to admit Dost Mohammed with an armed party into the citadel.
That he should be made prisoner and Heraut occupied was no
more than Shah Mahmoud had provided for ; but Dost Mohammed went much further.   He broke into the Zenana, or women's
apartments belonging to the Hajee's son ; and dishonoured the
wife of that prince, in other words, Mahmoud's daughter. Such
an outrage could not, of course, be forgiven ; and as Mohammed
effected his escape, Futteh Khan was charged with having suggested the offence ; and being seized by Prince Kamran, the
son of Mahmoud and the brother of the ill-used lady, he
was, with circumstances of peculiar cruelty, deprived of his
sight.

" The shout of Vizier Futteh Khan," says an able writer,
" as the knife of the executioner was thrust into his visual organs,
was that of the expiring Afghan monarchy."   All his brothers
heard of the deed with horror ; and they who had been un-
feignedly indignant with Dost Mohammed, and, some in pretence,
others in reality, had joined in pursuit of him, took up arms in
order to avenge the wrongs of the blinded man.   They made peace,
moreover, with the fugitive ; who, being beyond comparison their
superior in talent, soon acquired an ascendancy over them.   It
does not, however, appear that their designs extended further
than the deposition, perhaps the death, of Mahmoud, and the
setting up of another branch of the Suddozye family in his room ;
nor had they so much as agreed among themselves as to the individual who should be raised to the throne.   But the plans and
arrangements of men of inferior genius are everywhere bent by
a master spirit to its own purposes ; and hence Dost Mohammed,
partly by fraud, partly by violence, succeeded in thrusting the
house of Suddozye wholly aside   It is due to the character of

Shah Shujah to state, that in the midst of the troubles incident on this systematised rebellion, he made another attempt to recover the crown of Cabul. He was, however, deceived, betrayed, and finally defeated, and escaped once more to Loodianah, where for many years he dwelt peaceably in the bosom of his family.

While the civil war went on, Futteh Khan was barbarously hacked to pieces by order of Shah Mahmoud and his son Kamran. The cruel deed served but to exasperate the Baurackzye brothers, who, sometimes uniting their strength, sometimes acting independently, overthrew in all quarters the representatives of the rival house. They then began to quarrel among themselves, till at last the star of Dost Mohammed rose above the others, and he found himself master of Cabul and Ghuznee, and in a condition to give the law, in some sort, to his relatives. But the authority thus wielded was much more nominal than real. The several chiefs pursued each his own course, uniting with him whom they yet acknowledged as their head, only when great and pressing occasions required. Nevertheless, the progress made by the Dost towards the re-establishment of the Doorannee empire, though slow, was steady. He gained ground upon his rivals day by day; and whether through fear, or because they hoped for rest under his strong government, the city of Cabul, with the provinces immediately dependant upon it, paid to him willing obedience. He steadily refused, however, to assume the title of Shah, alleging that he had no treasure, and that a king without money was the most helpless of human beings. Nor were his scruples in regard to this point overcome to the last. Shah Shujah made, in 1834, his final effort, single-handed, to regain the position from which he had fallen. He was joined by many Rohillas, Seikhs, Hindostanees, and men from Scinde, and advanced as far as Candahar, to which he laid siege. There Dost Mohammed attacked him, and after a battle which seems to have been strangely mismanaged on both sides, gave him a total defeat. Shujah fled once more to Loodianah; and Dost Mohammed permitting himself on the field to be saluted as Amir, exercised henceforth more than kingly authority in Cabul.

CHAPTER III.

Early Negociations with Afghanistan—Preparations for its Invasion.

Ever since the foundations of British power in the East were laid, there has been more or less of intercourse between the rulers of Cabul and the representatives of the British government. For a while, indeed, this seems to have been on our part the effect rather of our fears, than of a higher motive. Nadir Shah had left a terrible name behind, which Shah Ahmed did his best to emulate; and in Shah Zemaun's time it was found necessary to assemble an army of observation on the frontier, lest the Afghan should march, as he had engaged to do, to the assistance of Tippoo Saib, with whom the Anglo-Indian empire was then at war. There followed this movement repeated missions—now to the court of Persia for the purpose of negotiating a diversion, as often as an inroad of the mountaineers towards Delhi was apprehended—now to Cabul when the prevailing cause of alarm chanced to be, that the French would contract an alliance with the Persians, and pass, by their help, through Central Asia, to the invasion of British India. It is not necessary to particularize the whole of these, nor yet to describe in detail the results to which they led. Enough is done when we state, that either because of the diplomatic skill with which they were managed, or that the dangers which they were designed to obviate proved more imaginary than real, the territories of the English in India have suffered no violation, though they have been continually extending themselves, and bid fair ere long to comprehend the entire Peninsula, from Cape Comorin to the Indus.

As the fear of invasion subsided there arose a laudable ambition to enter with the natives of Central Asia into more intimate commercial relations. The opening of the Indus to the trade of England and of British India was especially desired, and it was proposed in 1832 to communicate upon this subject with the governments of those countries, which from their local situation had it mainly in their power either to forward or to retard, if not entirely to frustrate, the arrangement. There were three such states, of unequal magnitude, which interposed at this time between the frontiers of British India and the river. The Punjaub, extending as far as the Hindoo Cush from the point, where the waters of the Sutlej join those of the Indus, obeyed the authority of Runjeet Singh, a successful adventurer, and an able though unprincipled chief, between whom and the British government a treaty of amity subsisted. The Punjaub was joined, and in part overlapped by Bahwalpore, a small principality which followed the course of the river downwards to about latitude 27°. And finally Scinde, over which a number of Ameers or petty princes held sway—themselves foreigners and nearly related to one another—took the line up and carried it on to the sea;—and the country on both banks of the Indus was thus far within their jurisdiction. With the heads of these several states treaties were entered into, which gave such promise of good that it was deemed advisable to push the matter farther, and to make a great effort—in the words of Lord Auckland, "to gain for the British nation in Central Asia that legitimate influence which an interchange of benefits would naturally produce."

With this view, or rather, to use the terms of the Simla proclamation, " with a view to invite the aid of the *de facto* rulers of Afghanistan to the measures necessary for giving full effect to these treaties," Captain Burnes was deputed towards the close of the year 1836, on a mission to Dost Mohammed Khan, the chief of Cabul. The progress of this mission, as well as the strange misapprehensions which induced the Envoy to withdraw from the scene of his labours at a very critical moment, are well known. A conviction seems, whether rightly or not, for some time previous to have matured itself in the minds of the local authorities, that peace with Afghanistan, so long as it should submit to its then government, was impossible. They had satisfied themselves that Dost Mohammed Khan was in friendly communication with the enemies of British power in the East. He was charged with having sanctioned the advance of a Persian army to Heraut, and to have connived at the siege of that place, which was then carried on.   It was laid to his door as an act of hostility towards England, that he had made an unsuccessful effort to wrest Peshawur out of the hands of Runjeet Singh, and was prepared to renew it.   And, finally, a Russian officer made his appearance in Cabul, and it was concluded that he came thither in order to make arrangements for the invasion, sooner or later, of British India, by the forces of the Czar.   We are not going to analyze the process of reasoning which led to these several conclusions.   It is sufficiently set forth in the document to which reference has actually been made ; and whether well or ill-founded, led to results which must long be remembered on both banks of the Indus, and, as will be made more apparent from day to day, are still only in progress.

There was to be war in disguise between British India, and the tribes which occupy the different provinces of Afghanistan. The object of this movement was not to be, on the part of England, the extension of her territory by conquests achieved in Central Asia ; but the restoration of peace to a country torn by civil dissensions, and the establishment in power of a prince well disposed towards a British alliance, and able and willing to counteract the objects of whatever states might meditate designs hostile to British interests.   Shujah Doulab-ool-Mulk was considered to be the individual marked out for the accomplishment of these important objects ; and though he had been repeatedly driven into exile, and now resided within the precincts of the English territories, " his popularity at home was said by the Governor-General to have been proved by the best authorities." It was accordingly resolved to espouse his cause.   " His Majesty Shujah-ool-Mulk," says the Simla Manifesto, " will enter Afghanistan surrounded by his own troops, and will be supported against foreign interference and factious opposition by a British army."   That the probabilities, both of foreign interference and of factious opposition, were calculated largely, the extent of the preparations esteemed necessary to defeat the one, and overcome the other, demonstrate.

The first step to be taken was to come to a right understanding with the powers whose territory intervened between the most advanced of the British posts, and the country in which it was proposed that the British army should operate. Under the management of Mr. MacNaghten, at that time Secretary to the Government of India with the Governor-General, a treaty was accordingly concluded, whereby Runjeet Singh undertook to co-operate with the British Government in the restoration of Shujah-ool-Mulk to the throne, on the understanding that the Maha Rajah should be left in possession of the provinces which, amid the troubles of late years, he had wrested from the kingdom of Cabul. We further know, from Lord Auckland's Manifesto, " that a guaranteed independence was, on favourable terms, to be tendered to the Ameers of Scinde; and that the integrity of Heraut, in the possession of its present ruler, would be respected. Thus on both flanks of his dominions, the legitimate king was to be cut short; for Heraut, being in possession of the son of Shah Mahmoud, would be as little subject to his sway in the west as Peshawur, now occupied by a Seikh garrison, would obey him in the east.

These points being settled, two corps d'armée were directed to assemble—one in the province or presidency of Bengal, the other at Bombay. The former, consisting of five brigades of infantry, one cavalry brigade, with artillery, engineers, &c., in proportion, was to be told off into two divisions; of which Major-General Sir Willoughby Cotton, G.C.B., K.C.H., was to command the first; and Major-General Duncan to command the second. The divisions comprised respectively the following regiments brigaded together, under the officers whose names are given :—

First Division of Infantry—three brigades.

First Brigade :—

COLONEL SALE, C.B., ... H. M. 13th Light Infantry.
{ 16th Regiment Native Infantry.
H. M. 13th Light Infantry.
48th Regiment Native Infantry.

Second Brigade :—

COLONEL NOTT . . . . 42nd Native Infantry.
{ 42nd Native Infantry.
31st Native Infantry.
43rd Native Infantry.

Third Brigade :—

COLONEL DENNIS . . . . . . {H. M. 3rd Buffs.

{27th Regiment Native Infantry.
{H. M. 3rd Buffs.
{2nd Regiment Native Infantry.
{One Company of Sappers.

Second Division of Infantry, MAJOR-GENERAL DUNCAN.

Fourth Brigade :—

LIEUT.-COL. ROBERTS . . . . Bengal European Regiment.

{35th Regiment Native Infantry.
{Bengal European Regiment.
{37th Regiment Native Infantry.

Fifth Brigade :—

LIEUT.-COL. WORSLEY . . . . 28th Native Infantry.

{ 5th Native Infantry.
{28th Native Infantry.
{53rd Native Infantry.
{One Company of Sappers.

The cavalry brigade, of which Col. Arnold, H. M. 16th Lancers, was at the head, mustered :—

2nd Regiment Light Cavalry.
H. M. 16th Lancers.
3rd Regiment Light Cavalry.

The artillery, commanded by Lieut.-Col. Graham, Bengal Horse Artillery, comprehended :—

2nd troop, 2nd brigade, Horse Artillery.
3rd troop, 2nd brigade,   ditto.
3rd company, 2nd battalion.
4th ditto   ditto.
2nd company, 6th battalion.

The collective regular force set apart at Bengal for service across the Indus may be estimated at ten thousand men. Meanwhile Bombay was gathering together its corps under Lieut.-General Sir John Keane, which, consisting of two infantry and one cavalry brigades, with artillery and engineers, could not

fall much short of six thousand men.   The regiments employed
were :—

First Infantry Brigade :—

COL. WILTSHIRE,
Lieut. Col. H. M. 2nd } H. M. 2nd, or Queen's Regiment.
19th Regiment Native Infantry.
H. M. 17th Regiment.

Second Brigade :—

COL. GORDON . . . . 1st Regiment Native Infantry.
2nd   ditto   ditto.
5th   ditto   ditto.

The cavalry, consisting of two squadrons, H. M. 4th Light
Dragoons and the 1st regiment of Light Cavalry, was commanded by Lieut.-Col. Scott, of the 4th Light Dragoons; while
at the head of the artillery, nearly two troops of horse artillery
and two companies of foot artillery, Col. Stevenson was placed.
Both corps, it is worthy of remark, were attended by bodies of
irregular horse.   The Poonah auxiliaries, as they were called,
accompanied the column from Bombay, while the Bengal column
was attended by a force of which, for obvious reasons, it is necessary to give a somewhat more detailed description.

It was the policy of the British government to speak on all
occasions of the inroad into Afghanistan as the effort of a de-
throned sovereign to recover his rights, and of the part played
in it by their own troops as that of mere auxiliaries.   An army
of his own was therefore essential to the dignity of Shah Shujah;
and as he does not appear to have had a single Afghan near him,
measures were taken to supply the deficiency from a different
quarter.   Inducements were held out to the followers of the
British camp, to wandering Beloochees, Seikhs, and men of every
tribe, to enrol themselves as soldiers of the King of Cabul; and
about eight thousand, tolerably well armed, but of course altogether undisciplined, were got together.   Of these the son of
the Shah, the Shezada Timour, as he was called, nominally took
the command, the charge being entrusted, in point of fact, to
Col. Simpson, of the 19th Native Infantry.   There attended
them a distinct staff, a commissariat, and a military chest.
Thus the outward show of that native force which the soldiers

of the Company were informed that they were to accompany and
sustain, was provided, while the whole cost and care of paying,
victualling, and transporting the same devolved upon British
agents and the British treasury.

The plan of campaign had arranged that while the Bombay
column, proceeding by sea to the mouth of the Indus, should land
there and operate upwards to Sukkur, and thence over the table-
land of Belochistan and the Bolan Pass upon Candahar, the force
from Bengal should concentrate at some convenient point near
the frontiers of the Punjaub, whence it might move upon Peshawur, and traverse the Khyberee Hills, and proceed by Jellalabad
and the Tezeen Valley to Cabul.   Difficulties both columns
were expected to meet; for it was known that the roads were
bad, and the tribes inhabiting the mountain-ranges fierce and
hostile; but the friendship of Runjeet Singh being secured, and
that of the Ameers of Scinde taken for granted, the possibility
of a repulse or a disaster appears never to have been contemplated.   Accordingly, during the months of July, August, and
September, troops marched by regiments and squadrons from
very distant points upon Simla, where a camp was formed, and
the Governor-General joined it.   Here General Sir Henry
Fane, who had been requested to undertake the command of the
expedition, issued his first general order, and here also was
published the document which, in the form of a manifesto, was
intended to inform the world in general, and the countries of
the East in particular, for what reasons the representatives of
the Honourable Company of Merchants, whose office is in Leaden-
hall-street, had assumed an attitude so hostile towards their un-
offending neighbours.   Then followed reviews, further orders,
the distribution of the force into corps and brigades, and, in due
time, an advance upon Ferozepore, where, in the course of the
latter days of November, the whole were assembled.

The friendship of semi-barbarous princes is not much to
be relied upon; and Runjeet Singh, the ancient ally, as he was
called, of the British nation, proved no exception to the rule.
He assembled, it is true, fifteen thousand men, with which he
proposed to support the Shah's troops, and exchanged entertainments, reviews, and diplomatic conferences with his allies;
but he declined to, permit the march of the latter through his

dominions, or the establishment of a place of arms at Peshawur. This was vexatious enough, yet the annoyance did not befal single-handed; for while the army was still moving up the rear of its strength to Ferozepore, intelligence came in, which, had it arrived three months earlier, might, perhaps, have obviated the necessity of assembling the force altogether. The Persians, it appeared, had raised the siege of Heraut; and thus the fear of opposition to Shah Shujah from without could no longer be pleaded as an excuse for the advance of more than his own followers into a country where his arrival had been stated to be looked for with impatience. What was now to be done? Abandon an enterprise, on the wisdom of which the judgment of so many had been declared, and permit an army to return without striking a blow, such, in point of efficiency and splendour, as British India had never before brought together? The idea was not to be entertained. Besides, who could tell what amount of duplicity might be hidden behind this sudden retreat of the Persians into their own country? They might have retired only to recruit their numbers, or to await the arrival of a Russian reserve; or the movement might have been made for the single purpose of deceiving us into the relinquishment of our designs. It was not, therefore, considered becoming to stop short of the re-establishment of Shah Shujah on his throne. Nevertheless, as the prospect of resistance was not now what at one period it seemed to be, a corresponding diminution in the numbers of the auxiliary corps to be employed was determined upon; and Sir Henry Fane, whose health was, moreover, infirm, resigned the command.

Under this change of circumstances it was determined to send across the Indus only three brigades of infantry from Bengal, namely, the first, second, and fourth, with two troops of horse artillery and a battery of nine-pounders. In the strength of the regular cavalry no alteration was made; and the whole, now regarded as a single division of the army of the Indus, was placed under the orders of Major-General Sir Willoughby Cotton. A route, moreover, was assigned to it down the course of the Gharra as far as Sukkur, where, having formed a junction with the Bombay column, it was to cross the Indus, and penetrate, by way of Candahar and Ghuznee, upon Cabul. Well, and with

exceeding order, the movement was accomplished. Shah Shujah's
contingent led the way, keeping two or three marches a-head of
the British troops; the British troops followed by brigades at
short intervals, and, the Rajah of Bhawalpore proving faithful to
his engagements, supplies were found in abundance at every stage.
It was not exactly so after the border line of Scinde had been
passed. The Ameers, relishing the presence of the English in
their villages as little as they approved of the threatened re-an-
nexation of their territories to the Doorannee empire, exhibited
as hostile a temper as prudence would sanction, and failed to
furnish either forage or provisions, except in insufficient quanti-
ties. Nevertheless, the columns moved on, the men's pressing
wants being provided for by the activity and skilful management
of their own officers: and it was found, when the day of halt
arrived, that, except through the desertion of some of their
camp-followers and baggage animals, no loss whatever had been
sustained.

A good many camels, particularly of those attached to the
cavalry, had died or disappeared during this march; and recourse
was had in consequence to water-conveyance for a portion of the
baggage. This was an arrangement which did not promise much
with reference to future operations, neither were the prospective
difficulties of the campaign diminished, when it was ascertained,
soon after the arrival of the advanced guard in front of Bukkur,
that a feeling decidedly hostile had begun to manifest itself among
the Ameers. The Bombay division, it appeared, had not made
good its landing without opposition. The shipping had been fired
upon by an inconsiderable fort which commanded the mouth of
the Indus, and the admiral, in self-defence, had been obliged to
reduce it to ruins. Moreover, after the debarkation was effected,
the absence of all means of transport, except such as the ships'
boats could afford, kept the force many days stationary. At
length the column set forward, and on the 28th of December Sir
John Keane established his head-quarters at Tatta. But here
again fresh difficulties arose. The Ameers refused to furnish a
single beast of burden; they impeded as much as possible the
bringing in of grain and other supplies, and drawing towards
Hyderabad about twenty-five thousand men, assumed an attitude
of decided hostility. There was no longer an alternative as to

the course which the British army must pursue. Sir Henry
Fane, who was proceeding towards Bombay by water, and descending the Sutlej to the Indus, kept parallel with the Bengal
column, recommended that the latter should detach a force for
the purpose of co-operating with the Bombay division, and com-
pelling the Ameers to pay more respect to their engagements.

It may be questioned *now* whether the interests of British
India would not have been better served had the struggle, which
at one period seemed to be inevitable, taken place. There could
be no confidence, and there was none, between the English
government and the Ameers from that day forth ; and the latter,
as it was subsequently ascertained, had communicated their suspicions to several chiefs on the further side of the Indus.
Nevertheless, as the active exertions of Col. Pottinger, and
the friendly disposition of the Rao of Cutch, succeeded in
laying the storm for the moment, all parties seemed to rejoice.
Then came camels sufficient to transport imperfectly the more
necessary baggage of the Bombay column. They were procured
from Cutch at a very critical moment ; and Sir John Keane,
who had delayed only till they should arrive, forthwith began
his upward march.

Meanwhile the Bengal column, including Shah Shujah's contingent, was making its way steadily toward the field of future
operations. The Shah, with his durbar, crossed the Indus at
Shikarpore, and pitched their tents at Sarkhanny, on the opposite bank. The British troops encamped under the walls of
Roree, that they might cover the construction of a bridge of
boats, and thus secure their own communications with the rear.
The spot which the engineers selected as suitable for this purpose was an island in the centre of the stream, which the fortress
of Sukkur occupies ; and of this the previous treaty with the
Ameers had provided that the English should obtain temporary
possession. But it is one thing to sign a treaty, and another to
fulfil it.

CHAPTER IV.

Passage of the Indus—March upon Candahar.

OF the alarm of the Ameers, and their anxiety to evade the fulfilment of the treaty into which they had been drawn, it is not
the business of the present narrative to speak.   Long and by
various crooked methods they endeavoured to protract the surrender of Bukkur, a stronghold upon a rock in the middle of
the Indus, which, as forming a convenient place of arms, the
officer commanding the British army was directed to occupy.
But they yielded at length ; and with country boats and planks,
mostly sawn from the date-groves near at hand, the Indus was
bridged.   Meanwhile, however, the intelligence which came in
from the Bombay column retarded the passage of the army.
The Ameers of Lower Scinde evinced day by day a more hostile
disposition, and Col. Pottinger, having fairly announced to them
that the arrears of tribute due to the sovereign of Cabul would
be exacted, they charged the British government with bad faith,
and avowed their determination to fight it out.   Of course the
navigation of the Indus was stopped.   With Hyderabad commanding its course, and armed to resist the passage of vessels
bearing the English flag, it had become alike impossible for Sir
Henry Fane to prosecute his voyage, and for any portion of
the force from Bombay to ascend to Roree.   Accordingly Sir
Henry Fane landed, and, once more assuming the command of
the army of the Indus, directed a brigade of cavalry, with two
brigades of infantry, to advance against the refractory city and
subdue it.   The troops had not, however, approached within
sight of Hyderabad when it was announced by a despatch from
General Keane that the Ameers had submitted.   An immediate
return to Roree took place, and the Bengal column crossed the
Indus.

Doubts had been entertained in many quarters how far the

sepoys would pass with alacrity a river which Hindoos regard as the appointed limit to their wanderings. These were now dispelled; for the native regiments, one by one cheering as they went, marched across the bridge, and seizing the drag-ropes of the field artillery, drew the pieces after them. Indeed, the passage of the Indus is described by those who witnessed it to have been a military spectacle of the most imposing kind. The battering train and heavy shot were towed from one bank to another on rafts. The cavalry crossed on foot, each man and officer leading his horse on the left; the infantry, with their measured tread, caused the planks to sway to and fro; and last of all, protected by a strong rear guard, came long lines of camels. Several days were of necessity required to accomplish this important operation; for though the number of fighting men did not exceed ten thousand, the whole body of people, including followers and servants, could not come short of six times that number. And hence, though the leading brigade passed on the 14th of February, the 20th had arrived ere the whole force was concentrated round the head-quarter tent at Shikarpore.

The entire breadth of Cutch Gundava, from the right bank of the Indus to Muhesir, on the Bolan river, is a plain. Little herbage covers it for a space of twenty-seven English miles, and in the centre it degenerates into a sandy desert. No vegetation, beyond here and there a sprinkling of wild caper, and other shrubs of the sort, relieves its barrenness; and water is to be procured only at such pits or wells as travellers and caravans may have dug for their own use, and abstained from filling up again after they had refreshed themselves. To march a single column of ten or twelve thousand troops, with beasts of burthen and swarms of followers, over such a country as this, is clearly impossible. By small detachments only can an army make head, and by small detachments the British force was on the present occasion carried forward. The cavalry led the way. Infantry by brigades, and guns as they could be most conveniently transported, followed. No loss among the armed men was experienced; but camels and other beasts of burthen dropped and died in considerable numbers; while the hostile disposition of the inhabitants soon began to show itself in the attacks which they made upon stragglers and baggage.

D

The march across this plain having been successfully accomplished, a brief halt occurred, in order that time might be
given for closing up the rear, and collecting on the proposed
line of future operations such supplies as by purchase or otherwise might be procurable.   This done, the column again moved
on through some difficult ravines as far as Dadur, where Sir
John Keane, who had conducted the Bombay contingent up the
left of the Indus to Sukkur, opened a communication with it.
A few changes took place in the disposition and command of
the several corps by his direction.   Sir Willoughby Cotton, for
example, was placed permanently at the head of the Bengal division; Brevet Major-Gen. Wiltshire at the head of that from
Bombay ; and the commissariats of both being so organised as
that they might support without ever crossing or clashing with
one another, preparations were made for threading the Bolan
pass, not far from the mouth of which the tents of the Bengal
portion of the army were already pitched.

The pass or rift which constitutes the only approach from
Cutch Gundava into the great valley of Shawl, winds for a
space of about sixty miles among the Brahoiek mountains, and
carries the traveller, by a wild and desolate road, to an extreme
elevation of about 5000 feet above the level of the sea.   It
varies, in regard to width, from several miles to thirty or forty
yards, now opening out into wide glens, now narrowing into
mere gorges, which seem in their windings as if they would block
up from time to time all further means of progress against the
wayfarer.   The hills on either hand are abrupt and perpendicular,
being principally formed of the pudding-stone rock ; and through
the gorge runs a river, which in the dry season nowhere exceeds
two feet in depth, but which, in heavy rain, and during the
melting of the snow, is liable to be swollen into a torrent.   As
may be guessed, the road is little better than a waving line of
pebbles, across which, seeking out declivities wherever it can,
the stream passes perpetually ; while the banks are composed
entirely of huge boulders or loose stones, which the waters have
rolled downwards in their might and left to settle as their
strength receded.   Such a pass, overlooked in all its narrower
veins by clefts, among which marksmen may stand, and high
precipices, from the summits of which loosened rocks may be

hurled, presents to the eye of the soldier no common appearance. If defended by a handful of resolute men, the largest army that ever took the field would in vain strive to force it : for a few traverses would effectually block the mouth of the narrow gorges, and women, or even children, stationed on the pinnacles above, could, without the smallest danger to themselves, crush the column, while advancing to surmount these traverses, by rolling down huge stones upon their heads.

Such was the pass towards the mouth of which the leading column of the army of the Indus was now approaching ; and on the 15th of March, some hours before daylight, the advanced guard entered it. The force in question consisted of detachments of all arms—infantry, cavalry, and artillery. There was likewise a prudent intermixture of European with Native troops, the latter being found to work best, on all occasions, by the side of their more hardy comrades ; and, finally, the whole division was distributed, after the same fashion, into brigades, which were put in motion, with such intervals between, that one should never overtake, nor thus of course incommode, the other. It was calculated, that unless active opposition were offered, each brigade might manage to thread the defile in about six days ; and Providence favouring the expedition, the expectations of the leaders were fulfilled : for no enemy presented himself to resist the march, and the hardy enterprise was accomplished. But it was not accomplished without considerable anxiety, and some loss. Numbers of camels. unaccustomed to such journeys, dropped down and died. A furious storm of wind and rain assailed the troops while entangled in the narrow defile, and caused the river to rise so rapidly, that the corps of engineers, who led the van, had well nigh perished. Bands of robbers also hung upon the rear, cutting off baggage and murdering stragglers ; and of forage there was none, save such as the commissariat brought onwards with them. Nevertheless the exploit was performed without any serious detriment to the general efficiency of the army, and in due time the whole was once more concentrated under the walls of Quetta, a rudely fortified town in the province of Shawl, and the head of an inferior district.

There was grass and ghee for about a month's consumption with the force, when it broke up from Dadur. Little more than

a fortnight's supply remained when the tents were pitched at
Quetta. The hostile disposition of the inhabitants began likewise to make itself more manifest every day. Nobody brought
in supplies; and all the efforts of Sir Alexander Burnes and
other officials to procure them led to nothing. Mehrab Khan,
the nominal chief of Khelat, with whom a sort of treaty had been
concluded, hung back, and seemed indisposed, now that the
English were in the heart of the country, to execute its terms.
With the rear, likewise, communications could not but become
every day more insecure. Doubtless the advance of the Bombay
division would re-open the pass for a while; but supposing that
it should make good its progress as little harassed as the division
that preceded it, what good could arise? The moment the
entire army should have placed the Brahoiek mountains between them and the Indus, they must depend upon the produce
of the country, and the exertions of their own officials for subsistence: and whether these would suffice continued for some time
to be regarded as a problem as difficult of solution as it was
critical in its details.

It is well known that during the halt of the Bengal column in
the vicinity of Quetta, Sir John Keane with the Bombay force,
and Shah Shujah's contingent, struggled manfully to get forward
from Bukkur. He passed the plains without sustaining much molestation; but received no mark of kindness at the hands of any
one. As he drew towards the hills, likewise, the people seemed
better prepared to offer resistance than they had been while
General Cotton traversed their country. No army ventured, indeed, to face him in the field, but the system of plunder and
attack upon stragglers was carried on more vigorously than ever;
and on one occasion, in the Bolan pass, a valuable convoy fell
into the hands of the Belooches, the escort having been cut to
pieces. It was observed, also, that not a man of weight and
influence came to join the king. On the contrary, the few whom
considerations of policy had induced to seek his presence while
yet at Shikarpore, he had so disgusted by his coldness that they
returned to their homes, and spread abroad tidings every way
unfavourable. Neither was the intelligence received from the
front more cheering. At Candahar three brothers, members of the
Baurakzye family, were stated to be making vigorous preparations

for defence. The standard of the Prophet was about to be raised, and a holy war proclaimed; and every male capable of wielding a matchlock would be turned out to harass the Feringhees. But there was a good spirit in the British army. Already had the troops been put upon half rations, while the camp followers were reduced to a quarter of their accustomed supply; the forage, likewise, had been curtailed in similar proportions, till both cavalry and artillery had ceased, through the weariness of their horses, to be serviceable: yet not a murmur was heard in the camp; and when, on the 6th of April, orders were issued to continue the march, men and officers prepared to carry them into execution with equal cheerfulness and confidence of success.

On the 7th of April, at an early hour in the morning, the forward movement began. It carried the column, and its huge train of followers and beasts of burthen, through a very varied country; a wide plain, arid and barren, being succeeded by a gorge or pass, and mountain streams here and there interposing to the passage of the guns obstacles of no ordinary nature. The marches were in consequence short; yet the fatigue to man and beast proved excessive: for a grievous absence of supplies, water itself failing in many places, occasioned universal weakness, which is in all situations accompanied by more or less dejection of spirits. The mortality among the cavalry horses was great. Camels, also, lay down and died, or fell over precipices, and with their loads perished: while marauders hung upon the line of march, and committed many outrages. The progress through the Kojak pass in particular, a rift in the Khojeh Amram mountains, though less tedious, was to the full as difficult as the threading of the Bolan, and cost the army much baggage, especially in its descent into the farther plains, through the inability of the camels to hold their footing upon a track that was both steep and loose. Moreover, as the force was now in an enemy's country, and the talk of opposition became distinct, it was found necessary to conduct every operation with care. No more tents were sent forward, or pitched in time to shelter the troops, on their arrival, from the sun. On the contrary, the baggage moved in rear of the leading brigade, and was covered in its own rear by the Shah's contingent; and in the long column no further

breaks were allowed than the nature of the ground to be traversed rendered unavoidable.   Nevertheless no enemy worth
forming up to receive met them; and on the 26th, Candahar,
the ancient capital of the Doorannee empire, was reached.   It
was entered by the first brigade without a shot having been fired,
except at plunderers.   There had been much expectation on both
sides of a vigorous resistance ere Candahar should fall.   Three
brothers, who held it in a sort of feudal dependence on Dost
Mohammed, had collected a considerable force, and gave out, that
they should stop the invaders in the Kojak pass, and if worsted
there, try the chances of a siege.   Dost Mohammed, also, had
encouraged them to strike a blow by repeated assurances that he
would march to their support: but when the storm drew near
their courage forsook them.   One of their number made his
peace with Shah Shujah, whom he joined, bringing in his train
a retinue of two hundred horsemen.   The others fled, and, though
pursued by Sir Robert Sale as far as the Helmund, succeeded in
escaping into Persia.   Upon this both the city and the territory
attached to it submitted.   Shah Shujah caused himself to be
proclaimed; and on the plain in front of his palace, the British
army pitched their tents.   Then, the Bombay contingent having
joined in the highest possible order, the whole were reviewed;
and provisions being abundant, and supplies of all kinds
cheap, two months were devoted to obtaining the rest and
refreshment of which both men and horses stood by this time
greatly in need.

CHAPTER V.

March upon Ghuznee—Capture of the Place—March on Cabul.

THERE was no increase of good feeling on the part of the inhabitants towards the invaders. The province submitted, or appeared to submit, to the rule of Shah Shujah, but of enthusiasm in his cause no class of society exhibited a sign; while the bearing of all in their intercourse with the English was as hostile as ever. Markets were indeed established, and, on the approach of harvest, grain was sold at a price less exorbitantly dear than might have been demanded for it. But to stray to any distance beyond the precincts of the camp was never safe, and in more than one instance proved fatal to the parties indulging in it. Two British officers, who had gone to fish the stream, were attacked on their return home, and one of them, Lieut. Inverarity, of the 16th Lancers, was murdered. A party of the 13th light infantry, who had been tempted to drive the animals and cattle too far to graze, were set upon, and several of them wounded; while a body of not fewer than two hundred camp-followers, when endeavouring to make their way back to Hindostan, were betrayed, disarmed, and butchered to a man. In like manner every detachment which made its way from the rear, every convoy of treasure, ammunition, and stores, was compelled to fight its way through the passes, and suffered much loss, both in life and in baggage. Nor was this all; the health of the troops began to give way. Days intensely hot, with nights of considerable severity, told upon the constitutions of the men, worn down by a march of many months' continuance, and the hospitals became crowded. The horses and cattle, on the other hand, regained somewhat of their original condition, a circumstance not a little to be rejoiced at, seeing that the prospect of active operations was before them; for Dost Mohammed, nowise overawed by the progress which the English arms were making, continued to breathe defiance; and it was generally understood that, ere Cabul could fall, a great battle must be fought.

At length, on the 27th of June, the march upon Cabul began. Right in the way stood the fortress of Ghuznee, where two of Dost Mohammed's sons commanded, and which was understood to be occupied by a stout garrison of several thousand men; and as it was determined not to leave such a place in the enemy's hands, men speculated freely concerning the measures that might be necessary to reduce it; for, strange to say, the battering cannon were all parked in Candahar. Cattle to drag them had become scarce, and the inconvenience experienced in the progress from Shikarpore upwards was painfully fresh in the minds of the authorities. Wherefore trusting that neither at Ghuznee nor anywhere else the Afghans would run the hazards of a siege, the army, leaving its train behind, set out in three continuous columns to open the new campaign.

Few events worth recording befel while as yet the route lay through the territory of Candahar. No sooner, however, was the frontier passed, and the invaders introduced into the territories of the Ghilzies, than they were taught in various ways that they had a different race of persons to deal with; and that in all probability the opportunity which they sought would be afforded, of striking a great blow at an enemy not wholly worthless. The Ghilzies, as is well known, compose both a numerous and a warlike tribe. Their chiefs inhabit towers or castles that lie scattered in great numbers through the valleys, while the hills which overlook them abound with glens and deep recesses, whence sudden outbursts might easily be made on a line of march conducted otherwise than cautiously. There was no lack of caution, however, on the part of the invaders. Advanced guards and flank patrols did their duty well, and the rear was closed and covered judiciously; and as the marches were short, scarcely exceeding ten miles a day, both men and horses came in at the termination of each fresh and cool. Moreover, except by showing here and there a body of horse in their front or on their flanks, the enemy offered no semblance of opposition. Rumour was indeed busy, and from time to time the word was passed to be on the alert, because danger threatened. But none came, and the very road improving, and the country exhibiting increased

signs of cultivation as they proceeded, the march of our people
to the vicinity of Ghuznee resembled more a triumphal procession than the progress of invaders through a hostile territory.

It does not come within the scope of the present narrative to
describe in detail how Ghuznee was invested, or by what process
it fell. The tale has been told many times already ; and though
we cannot deny to the soldiers who accomplished the feat all
praise for their heroism, it is impossible to hide from ourselves the truth, that success in that enterprise was mainly attri-
butable to a combination of fortunate accidents. Had the
enemy suspected our purpose of blowing open the gate of the
citadel, there would have been no difficulty in rendering the
operation impracticable. Had they offered a more determined
and better organised resistance to the storming party, it seems
incredible that such a place could have been taken by assault.
Moreover, all things combined to favour the assailants ; and on
the morning of the 28th of June Sir John Keane found himself
master of a city which the Afghans and other nations of Central
Asia regarded as impregnable. It was well for the reputation of
the general and the safety of the army that the desperate throw
proved successful, for there was not a gun within reach wherewith to batter ; and long ere the train could be brought up from
Candahar, the failure of supplies must have occasioned the dis-
solution of a force on which, by open attack, all the armed men
in the province could have made no impression.

The booty found in Ghuznee was great : but perhaps the most
valuable portion of it came into the hands of the commissariat
in the shape of horses, and other beasts of burthen.

The cavalry and artillery, which had become well nigh inefficient, received, in consequence, a considerable remount ; and
the commissariat, as well as individuals, experienced much relief in
the supply of fresh baggage animals, which they were thus enabled
to purchase. Neither was it a circumstance without value, that
a brother of Dost Mohammed fell, as a prisoner, into the hands of
the victors. But the moral effect upon the minds of the surrounding chiefs, no language can sufficiently describe. From the
moment that tidings of the event reached them, they seem to have
given up the cause of the Dost as hopeless. One after another,
as the column moved onwards, they hastened to offer their sub-

mission, till at last Shah Shujah seemed to have solid ground for
boasting that he had not deceived his allies in the statement
which he made touching the enthusiasm with which his subjects
would welcome him back to his throne.

Ghuznee fell on the morning of the 23rd of July. On that
day and the following the wounded were gathered together, and
bestowed in hospitals; and on the 25th, after clearing the streets
of upwards of one thousand dead bodies, a sale by auction took
place of the residue of such horses and camels as remained, after
the cavalry and artillery had been supplied. In the course of
the three succeeding days, something like order was restored to
the place, and, two regiments of native infantry having been
appointed to hold it, the rest of the army prepared to march
upon Cabul. There had been much talk of Dost Mohammed's
determination to risk a general action in defence of the capital;
but when the hour of trial came, it was found that his people
would not support him. Accordingly the invaders moved on in
good order and cautiously, but opposed by no obstacles more
formidable than those which bad roads and a wild country
threw in their way.

Dost Mohammed took up a position so as to cover Cabul,
and brought into it the whole of his field artillery—twenty-
two pieces. These he felt himself obliged to abandon,
because his troops melted away from him ere a blow was
struck, and they were all, on the 3rd of August, taken possession of by the British army. Meanwhile the Dost's remaining brothers, one by one, deserted him. Other chiefs, likewise, with their followers, crowded to offer obeisance to the
rising sun: and the purposes of the invasion seemed about to
receive their accomplishment. But the Dost himself still kept
the field; and so long as he should remain at liberty, the throne
of Shah Shujah would never be secure. Accordingly, information
having been received that, at the head of about three thousand
men, he had commenced a retreat towards the Hindoo Cush, orders
were issued to pursue. But either because the leader in the pursuit,
—an Afghan renegade—betrayed his trust, or that the start of
the fugitive was too great, or the country to be traversed too difficult, the Dost was not overtaken. He managed, with his son
Akbar Khan, to penetrate into the recesses of the mountains,

and so to baffle, for a while, all the efforts of his enemies to circumvent him.

Meanwhile the army continued to advance, the Bengal column leading; while, from the side of the Punjaub, a large subsidiary force of mercenaries and Seikhs, under the command of Colonel Wade, pressed forward. This latter corps, which had been left at Ferozepore, when Sir Willoughby Cotton conducted the movement of the army of the Indus down the course of the river, had subsequently approached the Khyberry passes, through which, not unopposed by Dost Mohammed's favourite son, it made its way. At first, the obstacles presented to Colonel Wade were very formidable. Not only is the country difficult in a military point of view, but Akbar Khan, having his head-quarters at Jellalabad, was at the summits of the ravines, ready with the *élite* of his father's infantry, and with the whole of his guns, to overwhelm the invaders as soon as they should become entangled amid their ascent of the Khyber. The rapid progress of the army of the Indus, however, so alarmed the Dost, that he called his son and his artillery to the position which he had selected for the defence of Cabul, and the Khyberries being thus abandoned, except by straggling parties of marauders, Colonel Wade forced his way through them with little opposition. The consequence was, that as the main body approached Cabul from one side, Wade and his motley band drew towards it from another, and thus the whole escorted Shah Shujah with triumph to his palace in the Balla Hissar.

Thus far the plans of the Indian government seemed to be executed, and the most extravagant wishes of the promoters of the expedition fulfilled. Dost Mohammed was a fugitive; and Shujah-ool-Mulk sat on the throne of his ancestors. Of Russian intrigues and Persian encroachments mention had ceased to be made. Cabul and the fertile district around it appeared to be well pleased with the change of dynasty; and as the Shah's native army had swelled to a larger amount than either he or the chiefs of his allies appear at one time to have counted upon, the number of British troops which it might be judicious to leave in support of the new order of things, came at once under consideration. Some there were who conceived, that two brigades—one in Eastern, the other in

Western Afghanistan—would suffice to give to the Shah as much confidence as, from the presence of a foreign force, he could require. It was, however, only at the beginning of Dost Mohammed's flight, when his fortunes were supposed to be prostrated effectually, that this idea suggested itself; for by and by, when that indefatigable man was heard of as gathering round him partisans in independent Tartary, wiser counsels prevailed: and finally the resolution was arrived at, that for some time, at all events, it would be necessary to keep the country in military occupation; and that the whole of the Bengal corps would not prove too numerous to accomplish this object. Accordingly three brigades of infantry, with the 2nd regiment of Bengal Light Cavalry, and artillery in proportion, were told off for service to the westward of the Khyber; and Sir John Keane having made up his mind to return with the residue to the provinces, Major General Sir Willoughby Cotton was put in orders to command the whole.

CHAPTER VI.

Breaking-up of the Army of the Indus—The unquiet State of Afghanistan—
Surrender of Dost Mohammed.

IT was in the month of September, 1840, that the army of the
Indus broke up ; a portion of the force returning by the Khyber
pass and Peshawur, through the Punjaub, to the Bengal provinces ; another portion marching by Quetta, on Sukkur and
Upper Sinde. Sir John Keane accompanied the former division
in person ; the command of the latter devolved upon Sir Thomas Wiltshire, to whom likewise was entrusted the task of
punishing the Khan of Khelat for his treachery, and reducing
the province of which Khelat is the capital, to subjection. Sir
John Keane and his escort performed their journey with little
inconvenience, beyond that which the roads and a severe climate
occasioned. Sir Thomas Wiltshire fought a gallant action under
the walls of Khelat, carried the place by assault, and slew the
treacherous Khan ; and proceeded thence, commanding the
respect of the tribes through whose territories he passed, till he
reached the Indus.   Meanwhile the troops left to occupy Afghanistan spread themselves among the principal strongholds,
and took them in possession : they consisted, in addition to the
British regiments, of the Shah's contingent, thirteen thousand
strong, and of a corps of Seikhs, of which the aggregate amount
may be taken at three thousand five hundred. We shall not,
therefore, much overrate the strength of the army by which
Shah Shujah was supported, if we put down its total amount at
twenty thousand men. Unfortunately, however, little or no
dependence could be placed upon the Asiatic levies. Though
armed and paid by the British government, they had been
gathered in from so many different sources that the principle
of cohesion had no existence among them, and all, it was to be
feared, looked with equal distaste and abhorrence on the presence
of the Feringhees, or infidel Europeans, among them. The die,

however, was cast, and the throw was described by such as had
the largest stake in the game to be favourable.   So the Supreme Government of India rejoiced in the re-establishment of
the Doorannee empire, and took such measures as appeared necessary to consolidate and support this creature of its own
formation.

The original distribution of the British army was settled as
follows: H. M. 13th Light Infantry, and the 35th Native Infantry, with six field-pieces, besides the citadel-guns, were to garrison
Cabul.   They were to be supported by a regiment of the Shah's
cavalry, and some of his artillery; and the whole were to be
under the orders of Lieutenant-Colonel Dennie.   The 4th brigade, including the 48th Native Infantry, the 2nd Light Cavalry,
with a rassalah of Skinner's irregular horse, were to occupy,
with six guns, cantonments at Jellalabad.   Ghuznee was to be
held by the 16th Native Infantry, a rassalah of Skinner's horse,
and such details of the Shah's contingent as might be made
available.   The 42nd and 43rd Native Infantry were to be stationed, with some of the Shah's troops, and the heavy train, at
Candahar, and Khelat-i-Ghilzie was likewise occupied.   Thus
the total number of British regiments left in Afghanistan to
act in co-operation with the Shah's troops were one European
regiment, the 13th, seven of Native Infantry, one of Native
cavalry, with artillery.   Of the exact strength of these it would
not be easy to speak; but the total amount of armed men,
natives and foreigners included, could not fall short, as we have
just said, of twenty thousand, while of cannon there were, in camp
and in store, between seventy and eighty pieces.

It formed a remarkable feature in the manner of adjusting
these affairs, that not only was the King of Cabul supported on
his throne by British bayonets, but that there resided within his
dominions and about his court, a whole army of British political
agents.   It seemed, indeed, as if the British government had
not only distrusted his Majesty's military strength, but reposed
no confidence whatever in his sagacity or political firmness.
Moreover, one of the great principles of the English constitution, the subserviency of the military to the civil power, was
applied to a case for which it was altogether unsuited.   In a
country inhabited by a rude people, who, if not positively hostile

to the existing government, at least entertained for it no respect, where the evil to be guarded against was a military insurrection, and peace and order could be maintained only by the sword, all authority over the troops, both in regard to the choice of their positions and the manner of using them, was vested in civilians. Now, however politic this distribution of authority may be in a country where law is respected, and men know their proper relations to each other, a moment's thought must convince the least reflecting, that in Afghanistan it was wholly out of place. And it was the more likely to lead to confusion, that, out of these gentlemen in civil employment, almost all were military officers of a subordinate rank, in whom vanity and a mistaken confidence in their own supposed acquaintance with the science and art of war was pretty sure, sooner or later, to operate disadvantageously. The ablest member of the diplomatic body, Sir Alexander Burnes, early protested against the arrangement, and foretold the results to which it would lead. Neither in this, however, nor in other points hardly less important, were his opinions treated as they deserved; and the results will be remembered with sorrow and with shame as long as history shall survive to speak of them.

Had there been any fitness in Shah Shujah for the position to which he was raised, or any disposition among his subjects to conform to the usages of a settled government, the season of the year at which he began to reign would have offered great facilities for the consolidation of his power. The Afghan tribes, though hardy and enterprising, seldom undertake expeditions, predatory or otherwise, during the winter months. The climate is severe, and good roads being scarce in the country, which presents few features besides a succession of mountain-ranges, it is very difficult for either man or beast, amid deep snow, to accomplish long journeys. Hence Kaffelas or caravans never come or go during these months; and the collectors of the royal revenues, if they have not done their work already, must wait till the next autumn ere they set about it. There is, therefore, rest in all quarters—compulsory, no doubt, but so far favourable to the introduction of a good system of rule, that the minds of men are not pre-occupied; and they have leisure, if the inclination be present with them, to consider the tendency of the proceedings

of those set over them. Of Shah Shujah, however, it seems
now to be universally admitted that he possessed no natural
talents for command, nor any docility of temper which might
have been worked upon for good. He called to his councils
men obnoxious to the chiefs of tribes; he affected a degree of
state which not the chiefs only, but their followers, abhorred;
he went about and stayed at home surrounded by a body-guard of
Seikhs, Hindostanees, and strangers. No one was permitted to
approach him except with prostrations, and he displayed much
rapacity in the collection of his revenues. On the other hand,
the people fretted over the sense of defeat, and were outraged by
the prospect of a tyranny. The fear of British strength which
had at first overwhelmed them, soon gave way to impatience of
a British yoke; and plots began almost immediately to be
hatched, and a hostile disposition manifested. It was the conviction of these truths, forced upon him sorely against his will,
which induced Sir William Macnaghten, the resident at Shah
Shujah's court, to apply for a larger amount of British troops than
had originally been allotted for the occupation of Afghanistan;
and Major-General Sir Willoughby Cotton, after completing
his preparations for a return into the provinces, was forced in
consequence to resume the command till an officer of similar
rank should be sent to relieve him.

The first measure of the general naturally was to make choice
of a military position by which the capital might be overawed in
case an evil spirit should arise among its inhabitants, and at the
same time be protected against invasion from abroad. Now
the situation of Cabul is so peculiar, that, under ordinary circumstances, the course to be pursued in regard to this matter
could not be mistaken. There is but one commanding position
in or around the city, namely, the Chola, or upper portion of the
Balla Hissar. Crowning the highest points of two mountain-
ranges, at the base of which the town is built, this pile, half-
palace, half-citadel, not only overlooks and commands the tops
of the houses below, but is in itself of extent enough to afford
accommodation to three or four thousand men, with as much
ordnance, stores, ammunition, and provisions as would be necessary for a year's consumption. Moreover, such is the straggling
nature of the place, that the presence even of a strong garrison

would not of necessity interfere with any amount of room which the court while resident might require.   For the upper fort, or Chola Hissar, is quite distinct from the palace: it had been used from time immemorial both as a place of strength and as a state prison, and could scarcely be overlooked by the commanders of a British corps so entirely isolated as that of which Sir Willoughby Cotton had assumed the command.   Indeed, so obvious were the advantages to be derived from the occupation of the place, that while the army lay encamped on the Seeah Sung, or Black Rock, a hill of inconsiderable altitude on the flank of the city, artificers were set to work, who constructed within the fortress mud barracks, into which, as soon as they were completed, the 13th Light Infantry marched.   But the troops had not long taken possession ere the Shah began to complain that he was overlooked, and in an evil hour considera- tions of a misplaced delicacy were permitted to outweigh the requirements of military prudence.   Under these circumstances the 13th were commanded to evacuate the fort, and measures were taken to establish a fortified cantonment in a position, per- haps, of all that could have been selected, the most unsuitable for the purpose.

The Cabul river, taking its rise among the Taujeek hills, flows through an opening in the lower part of the Balla Hissar range, separating the city, with the Balla Hissar, from an extensive suburb, and by and by intersecting the gardens, orchards, and nobles' seats with which the city is everywhere surrounded. Outside this suburb, on the left of the river, the entrenched camp was established, occupying a piece of low swampy ground, which was commanded on all sides by hills.   There were forts or towers likewise, so planted that one or more overlooked each of the circular bastions by which the British lines were protected; and the lines themselves, measuring a thousand yards by six hun- dred, were rendered still less defensible by crowding in upon them the mission residence with its garden and offices innume- rable.   Moreover, the more to convince the people that by their conquerors they were neither feared nor suspected, the principal magazine or store, both of provisions and ammunition, was not so much as brought within the intrenched camp.   On the contrary,

E

an old fort, quite indefensible, and detached from both the cantonment and the Balla Hissar, was filled with stores, on the safety of which the very existence of the army depended ; and a hundred sepoys, commanded by a subaltern officer, were considered adequate to protect them. It has been argued, in extenuation of these gross military blunders, that here, and only here, could the road from Kohistan be covered : but surely even this excuse is inadmissible; for a camp which is itself commanded by heights, and overlooked by towers, cannot command anything, and is wholly worthless for the preservation of order in a city, from which it is cut off by a river. For though the Cabul river be bridged, it is at a point on which no sane man would think of acting, namely, in front of a suburb, filled with flat-roofed houses, the fire from which would annihilate in an hour any corps that should venture to face it.

Whatever men's hopes might be of the ultimate establishment of settled government in Afghanistan, they were not slow in receiving proof that, if effected at all, the much-desired end could be brought about only by slow degrees and incessant exertion. Scarcely was the site of the cantonment marked ere hostile movements on every side called away the troops from the labour of fortifying their own position to attack an enemy in his. Between Candahar and Cabul a fierce spirit of disaffection prevailed. There the warlike Ghilzies were up and doing; nor were they quieted, even imperfectly, till after repeated conflicts and considerable loss on both sides. Meanwhile Dost Mohammed, having baffled the pursuit of Major Outram, was heard of in Kohistan, where the inhabitants flocked to his standard. It was considered necessary to act offensively against him, and for this purpose a thousand Afghan horse, with six hundred infantry, marched upon Bameean : there they halted till the beginning of October, when a brigade of native infantry, with cavalry and guns, joined them. A smart action followed at a place called Syghen, a village thirty miles in advance of Bameean, on the road to Independent Tartary. It ended in the defeat of the Dost's adherents, and led to his retreat into Bokhara, where it was in due time ascertained that foul treason had been enacted towards him. He was seized by the king, and cast into prison; and as the idea of his escape seems nowhere to have been entertained, the Shah Shujah and his allies gathered up their courage again, and felt themselves secure.

It was an old custom with the kings of Cabul to spend the winter months at Jellalabad; which, lying full three thousand feet nearer than the capital to the level of the sea, enjoys a milder and more genial climate. To play the monarch was Shah Shujah's passion; and he accordingly set out, as soon as the weather began to grow severe, for the winter residence of his forefathers. There he resided till April, 1841; neglecting business, giving himself to state and parade, and receiving no other proof of the spirit of obedience among his subjects than their reluctant payment of an inadequate revenue which foreign troops wrung out of them.

Meanwhile fresh grounds of anxiety and fresh causes of exertion were continually presenting themselves. The family of Dost Mohammed, consisting of two hundred and forty-nine persons, had, on the imprisonment of the Dost in Bokhara, given themselves up to the British government. They were stationed at Ghuznee as a place of safety, till it should be found convenient to escort them to Hindostan; and the fact of their being there may have probably gone some way to confirm Shah Shujah in a belief that from his rival no more hostile attempts were to be apprehended should he succeed, which nobody anticipated, in achieving his liberty. Dost Mohammed, however, by a finesse, which need not here be detailed at length, did manage to escape. He reached the castle of the Walla of Kholoom after encountering many hazards, and was well received by that chief, who dreaded the advance of a British force into his dominions, and who had already contributed by his remonstrances, and eventually by a not unsuccessful war, in softening the rancour of the king of Bokhara towards his captive.

Great was the sensation produced throughout Afghanistan when tidings of these events spread abroad. Akbar Khan, by far the ablest of the Dost's sons, was still at large. He had rejected all the offers of the British minister, preferring a life of rude independence among the mountains to the home of an exile in Loodianah, no matter how highly pensioned: and having struck more than one independent blow, he now hastened, with

his followers, to join his father's standard. Immediately in all
the districts between Turkistan and Cabul the royal functions
were by Dost Mohammed resumed ; and a holy war—a war of
extermination against the Kaffirs—was proclaimed.

Information of the Dost's escape from Bokhara reached the
envoy and minister on the 17th of July, 1840. On the 6th of
August it was reported that disturbances had broken out on the
Bameean frontier. On the 7th intelligence arrived that the Beloochees had risen in force, and repossessed themselves of Khelat.
By and by tidings of hostile movements from Heraut upon Candahar were received, which were soon followed by authentic accounts
of a defeat of one of the Shah's corps in Bajore, with the loss of
a gun. These were distressing rumours ; for they clearly indicated that, though the volcano on which the army of occupation
sat might be quiet for a time, its fires would never cease to burn
internally. Moreover, the Seikhs, or, at all events, that portion
of them which occupied Peshawur, and stood between Cabul and
the Punjaub, were beginning to exhibit a hostile temper. It
would be unjust towards the authorities in Cabul, civil as well as
military, to insinuate that they behaved otherwise than with
equal courage and address under the circumstances. The Seikh
chiefs were narrowly watched. Means of ascertaining the state
of public feeling both in the capital and in the districts dependent
on it were established ; of which, though, when particularized to
our western ears, they may sound both harsh and iniquitous, it
is impossible to deny that they proved to be effectual. They
soon settled the point that Shah Shujah had no party in the
country ; that everywhere men were ripe for revolt ; and that
the powerful tribes dwelling in Kohistan waited only for the
coming of Dost Mohammed among them, in order to join him
with fifty thousand armed men. It was a season for action, and
not for deliberation, and, inadequate as the force at his disposal
was, Sir Willoughby Cotton seems to have wielded it judiciously.

On the 5th of September it was ascertained that Dost Mohammed was advancing upon Bameean. He had been induced to
follow this route rather than that which led to Kohistan, by
forged letters sent to him by Sir Alexander Burnes, which represented the Kohistannees as universally hostile to him ; for
though he found it difficult to reconcile the contents of these

letters with the information which from other quarters he had
received, he did not consider that it would be prudent to discredit them.   All his movements were made, however, under a
veil of impenetrable secrecy.   Though large sums were offered
for intelligence, little, and that but partially to be depended
upon, reached the British head-quarters; and hence the Dost appeared before Syglan so suddenly that the force stationed there
judged it expedient to retire.   Meanwhile the troops at Bameean
were reinforced; and on the 17th of the month slept securely
under their tents in profound ignorance that the enemy were
encamped within three miles of them.   Next day Colonel Dennie
saw, to his surprise, at early dawn, the hills that overlooked his
position crowned by some hundred Uzbecks; and, putting himself at the head of a detachment, advanced to repulse them.
They fell back; and he found himself in the presence of the
whole of the Dost's army, numbering several thousand men.
There was no hesitation on Dennie's part.   He attacked and
overthrew the enemy, taking from them tents, baggage, kettle-
drums, standards, and the only gun that was left to the Dost,
who forthwith fled, his ally, the Wallee of Kholoom, deserting
him, and threaded his way towards Ghoree, whence, through
one or other of the defiles of the Ghordabund range, he resolved,
as a last chance, to penetrate into Kohistan.

While these things were going on, a second expedition had
been fitted out at Cabul, and sent, under the command of Sir
Robert Sale, to perform services as important, and not less trying,
to the westward.   It consisted of Her Majesty's 13th Light Infantry, not quite four hundred strong; of two companies, 27th,
and as many of the 37th Native Infantry; of two squadrons 2nd
Bengal Light Cavalry, a couple of six-pounders, and a nine-
pounder gun; to which by and by was added a regiment of the
Shah's horse, numbered as the second.   Sir Alexander Burnes,
in the capacity of political agent, accompanied Sir Robert Sale;
and on the morning of the 23rd of September they quitted Cabul.
Their first day's march carried them to a place called Khijah-
nowash, on the road to Askrai.   From thence they proceeded
leisurely, disguising their object as much as possible, by Jerbon
and Karrabagh, to Robat; thus threatening, so to speak, the
whole of the many defiles which, at short intervals from one

another, intersect the Ghordabund. But one of their purposes
being to reduce certain refractory chiefs, who occupied a number
of forts in and about Tootandurrah, they here made ready to
strike the blow. That the rebels should have permitted them to
ascend so far into the mountains without risking an action is
marvellous. The road which they traversed led sometimes along
the base, sometimes through narrow valleys between hills, which
rising, in sharp cones, to the region of perpetual snow, were
clothed to half their ascent with wood ; and many a spot presented
itself where a handful of resolute men might have kept their own
against an army. Except, however, by occasional long shots,
and here and there an attempt upon the baggage, the mountaineers offered no interruption to their progress, and left them
to enjoy two days of unbroken rest in the camp at Karabaugh.

The town, or rather village, of Tootandurrah, stands at the entrance of what is called the Ghordabund pass. It occupies the
uneven ground whence the steeps that close in the pass like a
wall spring up ; and besides being surrounded by garden-walls,
is defended by a fort, and has several detached towers near it.
A chain of these fortalices, each within musket-shot of the other,
and of the village respectively, stretches away towards the east.
One fort is particularly strong, and the rear, or northern front of
the whole position, is covered by a deep canal; while beyond is
a valley entirely covered with gardens. It was to the assault of
this formidable post that, a little before daybreak, on the 29th,
the column set forward, a stout advanced guard being pushed on
a-head, and flankers, where the nature of the country would
admit, thrown out.

As the troops drew towards the scene of action, it was ascertained that the enemy had made very judicious preparations to
receive them. A strong party was drawn up under cover of
some broken ground, so as to block the road; a second party
covered the hills to the west ; the forts and towers were all filled
with matchlock men ; and the whole, as soon as our people arrived within range, opened their fire. In a moment the column
broke into separate bodies; one of which, accompanied by the
artillery, cleared the hills, while another turned the flank of the
force which protected the village, and, driving all before them,
penetrated into two of the detached forts. A rush was now made

upon the village by the principal column, which entered in at the
double, and almost as quickly as the men could approach each of
them tower after tower was taken. The rebels were defeated
with great loss, while on the side of the assailants only one officer
and six private soldiers fell.

Having accomplished this service, and, at the suggestion of the
political agent, levelled the towers and forts with the ground, Sir
Robert Sale halted a couple of days to refresh and look about him.
He learned that at Julgah, a strong fortress considerably lower
down towards the plain, a refractory chief had established himself,
and he determined to strike at him, as he had done at Tootandurrah.   With this view, he moved on the 1st of October to Chu-
rikar, where a reinforcement of the Shah's cavalry joined him,
and, pitching his tents, gave out that on the morrow the homeward march would be prosecuted. Meanwhile the Shah's cavalry, the janbazees, and five hundred Doorannee horse, making
in all about a thousand cavalry, were ordered to march out at
midnight, and to proceed to Julgah, sixteen miles off, so that the
place might be invested before dawn. The cavalry thus far performed the part that was assigned them faithfully; and the infantry and guns following at an early hour in the morning, the
rebel chief was shut up in his castle. About noon, on the 3rd,
one twenty-four pound howitzer, three nines, and two sixes, were
got into position. They forthwith opened their fire, and for three
hours and a half maintained it with equal alacrity and precision.
But the materials of which the fort was built would not admit of
breaching. Heaps of soil peeled off, it is true, and, as far as ex-
ternal appearance could be trusted, filled the ditches; but behind
these ruins a thick rampart still showed itself, in which the balls
lodged without in any degree shaking it. Under these circumstances it was determined to try the effect of an escalade; and
two separate storming parties, each opposite what was called its
own breach, were formed.

There were no scaling-ladders with Sale's corps, neither had
he timber at his command for making them; but out of the dooly
poles—that is, the poles of the sort of litters on which sick and
wounded men are carried—his artificers soon constructed very
respectable substitutes for them. Supplied with these, the companies of the 13th, which had been told off for the service, sprang

forward; and, through a murderous shower of matchlock bullets, gained the crest of the glacis. To spring into the ditch and erect the ladders was the work of a moment; but, alas! the ladders proved too short: they sank into the soft débris on which it was necessary to plant them; and did not, by a considerable space, reach the top of the wall. In vain the gallant fellows sprang up. They were unable to reach or to touch the coping of the rampart with their hands, and being fired at from loopholes and windows, behind which their enemies stood comparatively secure, they dropped one after another. It would have been sheer murder to continue this contest, so the bugle sounded a retreat. But while the forlorn hope was retiring, several officers entreated Sir Robert Sale that he would permit them to try again at a point where the wall seemed less lofty, and he assented. Away they went, followed by their brave men, and again the ladders were tried, and found insufficient. Four officers only managed to crown the wall: not a man could follow; and these, after maintaining their insecure footing till the bugle had repeatedly recalled them, were forced to withdraw. It would be an act of injustice towards the brave, were the names of these gallant youths omitted from the present narrative. Brevet Major Kershaw, Lieutenant and Adjutant Wood, Lieutenant Edward King, and Lieutenant G. Wade, performed this feat; and two, Lieutenant G. Wade and Lieutenant, now Captain, Wood, survive to wear the laurels that they won. The other two died as soldiers should: Major Kershaw in the disastrous retreat from Cabul; Lieutenant King, as shall hereafter be described, at the fight of Tezeen.

Mortified, but nowise disheartened by the result of this endeavour, Sir Robert Sale encamped for the night in a ravine, after directing the cavalry to maintain a strict blockade of the place, which he was determined to attack with shells and a renewed cannonade on the morrow. Unfortunately, however, the bad spirit which pervaded other classes of society was busy by this time among the Shah's troops; and the janbazees, instead of hemming the rebels in, sent, as soon as it was dark, to inform the chief that he might pass through their lines, if so disposed. The chief, wondering at his past success, and not venturing to anticipate a repetition of it, gladly closed with the proposal; and the consequence was, that when on the morrow preparations for opening the batteries were in progress, the fort was discovered to be empty. Sale immediately took possession; and, like the towers about Tootandurrah, Julgah was rased to the ground.

The casualties altogether in Sale's brigade amounted to not fewer than fifty; and it was ascertained that the total amount of the force which had been opposed to them did not exceed this number. Nevertheless, no discredit attaches to soldiers whom walls neither to be broken through nor surmounted repulse. Moreover, the *éclat* of victory was so far theirs that they won the enemy's stronghold and destroyed it; after which, on the morning of the 6th, they again shifted their ground: for to Sale two objects, each distinct in itself, though both equally important, had been entrusted. He was directed not only to punish the refractory chiefs in the valleys of Ghordabund, but to watch and head back Dost Mohammed, who since his overthrow at Bameean was understood to be seeking some other route by which to penetrate into the Nijrow Valley, or to strike a blow at Cabul itself. Accordingly the column marched backwards and forwards; halting now here, now there, according as the spies informed them that the Dost was near at hand or far away; till at last, after a fruitless effort to come upon him with a body of horse, the whole, infantry, cavalry, and artillery, took up a position at Korabagh, on the road to the capital.

If Sale's brigade manœuvred skilfully, and endured, without repining, much fatigue and many privations, the movements of Dost Mohammed were to the full as remarkable. He threaded defiles, descended passes, only to scale them again; hovered on the outskirts of various places, and approached near enough to the British camp to put its inmates on the alert for a battle. Moreover, having the whole district in his favour, the Dost was enabled to baffle every attempt at surprise, and was not without his adherents among the followers of the Shah's standard. On one occasion a whole company of Kohistanees deserted to him, and serious apprehensions were entertained lest the remainder should follow the example. Nevertheless Sale relaxed in his exertions not for a moment. On the 17th of October arrangements were made for surprising the castle of Dervish Khan, one of the steadiest and most respectable of the friends of the ex-ruler; but after a long detour, for the purpose of concealing the object of the movement, the castle was found to have been abandoned, and the troops halted at a place called Baboo-kooshgur. Here, on the night of the 18th, a desultory fire was opened upon the tents; but it did no damage, and long before dawn the enemy, who had approached within one hundred and fifty yards of the sentries, retired.

The 19th brought up from Cabul the remaining eight companies of the 37th Native Infantry, with three additional nine-pounders. Thus strengthened, Sir Robert Sale determined to attack Kurdurrah, a village strongly placed under cover of the lower range of the Lughman mountains, where about a thousand insurgents were stated to have assembled, with a determination to keep their ground to the last man. And, indeed, had there been among them the same amount of daring as of subtlety, it seems hard to imagine how the post could have been won, except at a sacrifice of life almost too great for the purchase. In addition to the defences of Nature's formation on ground abrupt and broken, overhung by ravines innumerable, there ran between the villages of Kurdurrah and Brydack two miles of gardens and vineyards, the whole of which occupied terraces on the sides of the mountains, and were defensible to an extent which is to be understood only after ocular inspection; and, as a matter of course, each garden and vineyard had its tower or fortalice overlooking it. But the occupants of that strong ground were wanting in confidence one towards the other. The soldiers distrusted the peaceable inhabitants; the peaceable inhabitants looked with disfavour on the soldiers; and the consequence was, that during the night of the 20th the position was entirely abandoned: wherefore Sir Robert Sale, after burning the villages, levelling the towers, and destroying the gardens, marched back to Arksai, where he again placed himself in observation over Cabul.

It was well known by this time that Dost Mohammed had penetrated into the Nijrow Valley, and that the little band with which he arrived there was receiving daily accessions to its strength. Under these circumstances Sir Willoughby Cotton detached a force from Cabul, which, pushing by a forced march upon Istalif, took possession of it; while Sale, having remained stationary about a week, broke up once more, and manœuvred to strike at the Dost wherever he might find him. He proceeded first to Julgah, and thence upwards to Bigh-i-alum, sending his tents before him, as if his purpose had been to proceed somewhere by the route of Tootandurrah. But no sooner was he put in possession of accurate intelligence regarding the Dost's proceedings than he suddenly changed the line of his march, and passed on towards Prurwan Durrah. He traversed on this occasion a valley through which ran two rapid streams, both of them fordable, yet offering some impediments to the march of artillery; but his knowledge that the enemy was near, and that all the people round about viewed him with disfavour, compelled him to make his approaches carefully. On the 2d of November his advanced guard consisted of two six-pounder guns, two companies of the 13th Light Infantry, two flank companies of the 37th, and one of the 27th Native Infantry, two squadrons of the 2d Bengal Light Cavalry, and two hundred of the Shah's 2d horse. Lieutenant Colonel Salter commanded the whole; and for a while, in spite of the difficulties of the road, its progress was as steady as could have been desired. Doubtless here and there a fort fired upon the men, but there seemed little disposition among the inhabitants of the villages to swell the number of the Dost's followers, for they flocked in by the score, intreating protection against the invader, whom they described as plundering without mercy wherever he went. At last, from various tokens that presented themselves, it was judged that the Dost, with his corps, could not be far distant. The country people described the latter as 3500 strong; and held out hopes, that if a body of cavalry were pushed on by a route which they described, the retreat of the whole might be cut off. This idea, which Dr. Lord strongly confirmed, was acted upon without delay, and two squadrons of the 2d Bengal Cavalry were directed to skirt the hill on the right, while the left of the pass should be occupied by the Shah's horse. It is not necessary to describe in detail the mortifying results that followed. The 2d Bengal Cavalry, being threatened by about two hundred of Dost Mohammed's horse, turned and fled, leaving their officers to be cut to pieces; while the infantry, though they presented as usual a steady front, could not stop the enemy from effecting their retreat in good order. But the Dost went not with them. He had borne himself gallantly in the charge of horse. He had recovered marvellously from his defeat at Bameean, and could boast of as large a following as attended him previously. But he felt that for the present his game was played out. Accordingly, while his people marched back towards the Nijrow Valley, he stole away from them, with a single attendant in his train; and, taking a circuitous route, so as to avoid Sir Robert Sale's camp, pushed for Cabul.

On the evening of the 3d, the day succeeding the skirmish, Sir William Macnaghten was returning from a ride into the country, and had approached within fifty yards of the city gate. A horseman suddenly passed his escort, and pulling up his weary steed beside that of the envoy, announced that he was Dost Mohammed. Of all that followed it is unnecessary to speak. Dost Mohammed was graciously received and treated with much kindness. He was restored to his family, or, to speak more accurately, his family was restored to him; and the whole, being put under the charge of a sufficient escort, proceeded by Jellalabad, and through the Khyber Pass into the Punjaub, and thence to the place of residence which had been allotted to them within the Company's territory.

CHAPTER VII.

Peaceful Occupation of Cabul and the Posts adjacent.

So passed in this direction the summer and autumn of 1840. Elsewhere, likewise, success had attended all the operations of British officers; for Khelat was recovered, the Ghilzies were put down, the Beloochees reduced to an unwilling obedience, and the Seikhs of Peshawur overawed. Accordingly, at the approach of winter, Shah Shujah and his court retired, as they had done the previous year, to Jellalabad, where Sir Willoughby Cotton bore them company. Neither did aught befal between November, 1840, and the early summer of 1841 to excite serious alarm, or much suspicion anywhere. Kept down, partly by the climate, partly by the respect which they entertained for British prowess, the heads of the tribes lying to the north of Ghuznee remained tranquil; and as Candahar, with the provinces dependent on it, was held by General Nott and a competent force, the occasional predatory risings of the people between Ghuznee and that place were not much regarded. In one district, and only in one, a different spirit prevailed. The Nijrow chiefs not only continued to hold aloof from offering any sign of submission to the new order of things, but granted an asylum to all the restless spirits from other places whom discontent or the fear of punishment for crimes already committed induced to abandon their homes. It is well known that the condition of that district was neither concealed from Sir William Macnaghten, nor by him overlooked. On the contrary, he repeatedly urged upon the Indian government the necessity of reinforcing the army of occupation, so that Nijrow, as well as other suspected provinces, might be adequately garrisoned. But considerations of economy would seem to have weighed more at Calcutta than the representations of the envoy, for no troops were sent, and out of this neglect competent authorities have not hesitated to affirm that the disasters which subsequently befel the army of occupation principally arose.

The time at length arrived when it was judged expedient to relieve a portion of the force now on duty across the Indus, and to fill up the ranks of the regiments still kept there, with drafts from their depôts.   In pursuance of this policy, the 44th Queen's regiment, under the command of Colonel Shelton, quitted the provinces ; and being on its march to Jellalabad, passed the remains of the 1st Bengal European corps, which was escorting Dost Mohammed and his family to Loodianah.   By and by a fresh convoy arrived, bringing with it Major-General Elphinstone, to whom Sir Willoughby Cotton had already made the necessary arrangements for giving over the command.   The two generals seem to have passed one another on the road.   The one returned, covered with honours, to Hindostan, the other proceeded, in bad health, and in not much better spirits, to take upon himself a charge for which he was neither morally nor physically fitted.   Poor Elphinstone came at an unlucky moment.   Already was the temper of the people beginning to exhibit itself so uncomfortably, that Colonel Shelton found himself obliged to diverge from his proper line of march, in order to punish a refractory tribe in the Nazean valley.   The expedition proved successful, for not fewer than eighty forts or castles were demolished; yet it has never quite appeared of what particular crime the malcontents had been guilty, or whether the head and front of their offending might not be a refusal to pay tribute such as had, at no previous period, been exacted of them.   Colonel Shelton and the 44th did, however, their duty ; neither were they less energetic a little later in the season, when the hostile attitude of the Seikhs, let loose from the restraint which Runjeet Singh used to impose upon them, called for a demonstration from Jellalabad through the Khyber towards Peshawur.   But there was no fighting on that occasion.   Captain Broadfoot, with his convoy, scarcely a thousand strong, put on so bold an attitude, and maintained it with such steadiness, that the Seikh marauders feared to risk a struggle, and suffered them to pass.   The whole, therefore,—these fresh arrivals and Colonel Shelton's brigade together,—proceeded onwards without let or loss to Cabul.

Never had Afghanistan, or at least that portion of it which lies to the north-east of Ghuznee, appeared to enjoy more profound tranquillity than at this time. Cabul Proper, Jellalabad, Kohistan itself, and the districts adjacent to each of them gave, or seemed to give, willing obedience to the government. Candahar, likewise, with the whole extent of territory, from the desert to the Helmund, if not pacified, was quiet; while the tribes in possession of the passes, particularly the Ghilzies and the Khyberries, were at once mollified and rendered happy by the receipt of a sort of blackmail, which, to the amount of 8000l. a year, the British government paid to them as the price of protection to its communications. Nobody therefore dreamed of danger, or would have credited the report had it been made to him, that in any of these quarters the spirit of intrigue and deadly hatred was busy, yet the spirit of discontent was very busy throughout the whole compass of the Doorannee empire; and Cabul itself had already been the scene of plots and conspiracies without end. Moreover, so early as the month of May, Major Pottinger, who had been appointed political agent in Kohistan, reported to the envoy that all was was not well in the province. He requested that more troops might be sent, and proved to demonstration that a single regiment consisting of natives of the place, with three six-pounder guns, could not, even if the infantry were to be depended upon, put down an insurrection. But Major Pottinger was regarded as an alarmist, whose representations ought to go for nothing; so that the clouds were permitted to gather and thicken from day to day, till the storm burst which swept the whole might of the British army, and for a season, the prestige of the British name alike before it.

It will be borne in mind that, as far as British influence extended, the newly erected Doorannee empire was divided at this time into two military commands. One of these, having its head-quarters in the capital, embraced the provinces which may be said to be based upon the parallel of the Suffaid Koh, towards the south. Its great towns were Cabul, Ghuznee, and Jellalabad. Its territory comprehended the several provinces that lie south of the Hindoo Cush, north of the lower roots of the Suffaid Koh, and east of the Helmund as far as Peshawur. Two European regiments of infantry, Her Majesty's 13th and 44th; four of Native infantry, the 27th, 35th, 37th, and 54th of Bengal; four squadrons of regular Native cavalry; two troops of horse artillery; one nine-pounder battery, under Captain Abbott;—these, together with swarms of the Shah's forces, horse and foot, constituted the garrison by which it was held. And at the head of the whole was Major-General Elphinstone, so far at least as an officer, who is required never to act except on the suggestions of an envoy, or political agent, or civil chief by whatsoever title designated, can be said to command an army at all.

The other military district, lying to the south and west of the Suffaid Koh, was far more extensive, and therefore required, and had allotted, for its protection, a more numerous army. Its towns were Candahar, Quetta, Khelat, Dadur, Gundava, and the small but important post of Ghiresk, upon the Helmund. Here General Nott commanded, having his head-quarters at Candahar, with garrisons in Quetta, Kelat-i-Ghilzie, Killa-abdoolah, and Ghiresk. But in process of time, when trouble began to thicken, these detached posts were abandoned, and in the end only Candahar, Quetta, and Kelat-i-Ghilzie, were occupied.

With the proceedings of the army under the command of General Nott it is not the business of the present narrative to interfere. Enough is done when we state, that long before matters had come to a crisis around Cabul, Candahar and the provinces dependent upon it were in a flame. Repeated insurrections took place, and many sharp actions were fought, the whole of which redounded to the honour of the British officers and soldiers, Native as well as European. Moreover, the Shah's revenue, miserably inadequate at the best, could seldom be collected except by British officers at the head of troops; and it rarely happened that these fiscal movements failed of bringing on collisions, always exasperating, and sometimes disastrous. In like manner the chiefs in Kohistan, and indeed everywhere else beyond the limits of a few miles round the capital, could be induced to contribute towards the maintenance of the government only by force. And as the whole of the troops thus employed, whether following the British standard or serving under that of the Shah, were paid and fed at the expense of the Indian treasury, the pressure of the burthen began, ere long, to make itself felt. At last the supreme government at Calcutta began to complain. Repeated instructions were given to the envoy that he should practise a rigid economy in all departments of the state. It was proposed to diminish the amount of military force by which the throne was maintained; and the question was continually put as to when, in the opinion of the experienced, it was probable that British support might be wholly withdrawn. Sir William Macnaghten seems to have met these instances with temper and moderation, and every desire to fall in with the views of his superiors. He could not recommend that the force which kept the country should be diminished, unless, indeed, the resolution were taken to abandon altogether the policy which had raised Shah Shujah to the throne. But he promised to reduce its expenses to the lowest practicable figure, and began his system of entrenchment at the wrong end. Had he dispensed with the services of three-fourths of the political agents, by whom Afghanistan was absolutely overrun, the saving to the British treasury would have been immense, and the damage done to either government very slight. But this course he did not judge it expedient to pursue; and the consequence was, a step comparatively little worth as regarded the saving to be effected by it, though of incalculable mischief, inasmuch as it fanned into a flame the insurrectionary temper which had long smouldered.

The communications between the most advanced of the British settlements in Hindostan and the capital of the empire of which General Elphinstone was in military possession, were both difficult and insecure. Besides that, the territories of allies not absolutely trustworthy must be crossed,—each convoy as it arrived on the frontier of Afghanistan, whether it came from Peshawur or by the more circuitous route of Sukkur, found itself at the gorge of the first of a series of mountain passes, to traverse which, even when unopposed, was difficult; to force a way through which, in the face of a resolute enemy, must have been, except to an army at once numerous and well disciplined, impossible. Between Peshawur and Cabul lie first the Khyber, next Jugdulluk, then the Tizeen, and finally the Koord Cabul, all of them difficult, and the last long and winding, with a sort of basin or punch-bowl in the midst. On the other side, between the capital and Sukkur, there are all the ravines and difficult

F

places of which, while tracing with a rapid pen the advance of
the army, mention has been made; and of which one of the least
intricate proved, when attempted in an hour of danger, absolutely impracticable. Now two methods, and only two, were
offered to the envoy of keeping these passes open. They must
either be studded with strong military posts, whence not the
gorges alone, but the crests of the hills should be commanded
(and to accomplish this effectually would require an army); or
else the natives must be prevailed upon to do the work themselves. The latter course had been adopted, perhaps wisely;
and the Ghilzie chiefs, on consideration of receiving an annual
payment among the whole of them of 8000*l.*, agreed to protect
the march of convoys, caravans, and small detachments. Up to
the autumn of 1841, they fulfilled their part of the treaty with
greater exactness than, from the constitution of society in
Central Asia, might have been expected. But now it was determined to higgle with them about terms, and instead of 8000*l.*,
4000*l.* were offered. They indignantly rejected the proposal;
and from the hour when it was made, entered eagerly into the conspiracies which were everywhere maturing themselves round the
devoted general and envoy.

It has already been stated that in the month of May, 1841,
Major Pottinger, the political agent in Kohistan, communicated
to Sir William Macnaghten his fears for the peace of that
province, and urged that the military force allotted for its occupation should be increased. No great heed was paid to this re-
monstrance; nevertheless, a few native horsemen, with one gun
and a small reinforcement of the Shah's artillery, were sent to
him; and he was assured that the gentlemen at head-quarters
knew better than he how entirely without foundation were the
apprehensions which he cherished. Neither must we blame too
hastily the temper that led to a confidence which the progress
of events showed to have been misplaced. The Shah and his
counsellors evinced no signs of distrust. The city was quiet,
and so were the towns and villages dependent on it; and the
whole of General Elphinstone's command, with the exception of
the garrison of Ghuznee and one or two detachments less numerically strong, being concentrated round Cabul, it is hardly to be
wondered at if men, accustomed to give the law and to be

obeyed, should have discredited all rumours of a rebellion.
Accordingly, time appears to have passed, both with civilians
and military officers, pleasantly enough. The climate, though
hot, was less oppressive than that of Hindostan. The scenery
was attractive and the town full of good things ; and it rarely
happens that young men with swords at their sides look much
beyond the pleasant circumstances by which they may be surrounded. Hence a diary of the proceedings of most of them
would present, were it faithfully transcribed, an agreeable picture enough. There was society in the cantonments, for many
officers had been joined by their wives and families. There was
abundance of delicious fruit, and provisions were plentiful. Ex-
cursions to different points remarkable for their natural beauties,
or rendered memorable by the associations that were connected
with them, gave agreeable occupation both to mind and body.
And, to sum up all, it really appeared, judging from the manner
of the chiefs and the hospitalities which they seemed willing to
dispense, that whatever of antipathy might have existed on either
side towards the other when the acquaintance between the two
races began, was about to be supplanted by a better feeling. It
may not, perhaps, be uninteresting to the reader to be told how
his countrymen managed, during both summer and winter, to
kill time in the centre of Asia ; and the following account,
gathered from the journals of officers, may be taken by him as a
tolerably accurate detail of their proceedings.

CHAPTER VIII.

Peaceful Occupations at Cabul.

CABUL, as regards its general appearance, has been described, both by pen and pencil, too often and too accurately to warrant a repetition of the picture here. Houses, built chiefly of mud, with flat roofs, and surrounding, as in Spain, open court-yards; streets narrow and by no means remarkable for their cleanliness; bazaars or markets, each appropriated to its own particular use, wherein dealers of every description set forth their wares for sale,—these present in the capital of Afghanistan, as they do in most Oriental cities, the features which first attract the attention of the stranger. There was a wall, of course, carried round the city. Here and there the tower or castle of a chief rose above the ordinary level of the dwellings; and the Balla Hissar, crowning the rock which overlooked the whole, excited the admiration of the traveller, especially when looked at from a distance. But the mosques and other public buildings do not appear to have been very imposing, either for their size or the style of their architecture. In a word, intimacy had the effect in this instance which it is supposed to have in many others, of lowering to a marvellous extent the feeling of respect which a first acquaintance might have excited. Its position on an elevated plain, with tall rocks looking down upon it, and the Indian Caucasus with its summits of eternal snow forming the background to the picture, gave to Cabul, when first seen from afar, a very imposing appearance. It proved, when examined more closely and in detail, to be a mean collection of mean houses, and as filthy as all towns are which continue undrained, and are not provided with any of the conveniences which the habits of civilized men require.

It was in the beginning of August that the soldiers of England made their first acquaintance with this city. The orchards and gardens which surround it on every side were laden with rich fruit. The Cabul river flowed with a clear and rapid stream, fertilizing the plain and giving an air of gladness to the scenery. Inured to the climate and hardened by exposure, our countrymen seemed to regard the intense heat of the day as a trifle, and enjoyed the cool airs of early morning and the hour that followed sunset intensely. Throughout the whole of the autumn they lived under canvas, the officers passing to and fro with a confidence which, at this early stage of their acquaintance, appeared to command a like degree of honesty among the people. Of course, there was no lack of interesting occupation. Parties rode hither and thither to visit and inspect such objects of curiosity as were described to them. Baba Shah's tomb, of which Mr. Masson and Dr. Atkinson have both given a description; the obelisk, of which tradition ascribes the structure to Alexander the Great; the magnificent scenery about Arkserai, and as far into the mountains as it was deemed prudent to go, offered irresistible attractions to the admirers both of nature and of art. And when curiosity had begun to be appeased, other and not less characteristic modes of disposing of their time were by these light-hearted young men adopted.

Wherever Englishmen go, they sooner or later introduce among the people whom they visit a taste for manly sports. Horse-racing and cricket were both got up in the vicinity of Cabul; and in both the chiefs and the people soon learned to take a lively interest. Shah Shujah himself gave a valuable sword to be run for, which Major Daly, of the 4th Light Dragoons, had the good fortune to win : and so infectious became the habit that several of the native gentry entered their horses, with what success no record seems to have been preserved. The game of cricket was not, however, so congenial to the taste of the Afghans. Being great gamblers in their own way, they looked on with astonishment at the bowling, batting, and fagging out of the English players; but it does not appear that they were ever tempted to lay aside their flowing robes and huge turbans and enter the field as competitors. On the other hand, our countrymen attended them to their mains of cocks, quails, and other fighting animals, and, betting freely, lost or won their rupees in the best possible humour. In like manner our people indulged them from time to time in trials of strength and feats of agility on which they much pride themselves: and to their own exceeding delight, though very much to the astonishment of their new friends, they in every instance threw the most noted of the Cabul wrestlers.

The result of this frankness was to create among the Afghans a good deal of personal liking for their conquerors. The chiefs, in consequence, invited them to their houses in town, as well as to share in their field-sports when they retired to their castles in the country; and if the entertainments in the former situation soon grew heavy after the sense of novelty wore away, the latter appear to have been greatly relished to the last. And the accuracy with which the double-barrelled guns of the British officers brought down, right and left, snipes and quails on the wing, astounded those who never fired except at objects that were stationary. But greater marvels still awaited the Afghans.

The winter at Cabul may be said to set in towards the end of October. In 1839, for example, ice was seen in the ditches about this time of an inch or more in thickness; and as November and December advanced, the weather grew continually colder. No words can describe the intense delight with which men, long unaccustomed to the bracing air of a frosty day, hailed this change of climate; and when in January the snow began to fall, it seemed as if all the hues of summer were hideous in comparison with the uniform shining white wherewith the whole face of the country was overspread. Strange to say, however, the Afghans refused to believe that frost and snow were familiar to the senses of the Feringhees. They had marched from the burning plains of Hindostan; and the good people of Cabul, though aware that they were not Hindostanees, could not be persuaded to credit that they were natives of a cold climate. But this piece of incredulity our countrymen got the better of by a process as simple as it was ingenious.

There is a lake about five or six miles from Cabul, in the direction of Istalif, which, though partially saline, or rather metallic, in its waters, is frozen over in all winters if the weather be commonly severe. In the winter of 1839-40 it was covered with a coat of ice more than ordinarily thick, on which the Afghans used to practise the art of sliding, far more skilfully, as well as gracefully, than their European visitors. Indeed,

it was the clumsy manner in which the Feringhees assayed that
boyish sport which induced them to reiterate the conviction
that heat, and not cold, was the white man's element. Forthwith our young gentlemen set themselves to the fabrication of
skates : the artificers soon shaped the wood-work according to
models given ; out of old iron, smelted, and hardened afterwards,
the blades were formed ; and in due time a party of skaters,
equipped for the exercise, appeared upon the lake. The Afghans
stared in mute amazement while the officers were fastening on
their skates, but when they rose, dashed across the ice's surface,
wheeled and turned, and cut out all manner of figures upon the
ice, there was an end at once to disbelief in regard to the place
of their nativity. " Now," cried they, " we see that you are not
like the infidel Hindoos that follow you : you are men, born and
bred like ourselves, where the seasons vary, and in their changes
give vigour both to body and mind. We wish that you had
come among us as friends, and not as enemies, for you are fine
fellows one by one, though as a body we hate you."

Mention has been made of the hospitalities which were dispensed by Afghan chiefs to British officers. The latter were
not backward to return the civility. Not only the houses of
such men as the envoy, the commander-in-chief, and Sir Alexander Burnes, were thrown open to them, but the mess of the
13th received its frequent guests, most of whom ate and drank
with as much good will and indiscrimination as if there had been
no prohibitory clauses in the Koran or elsewhere. Among other
means adopted to entertain the aristocracy of Central Asia,
the British officers got up a play : a theatre was constructed,
scenery painted, dresses prepared, and excellent bands in attendance ; and as the pieces which they chose were chiefly broad
comedies, such as the ' Irish Ambassador ' and others of the
same sort, great amusement was afforded to the audience. For
on such occasions they changed the titles of the *dramatis personæ*,
so as to bring them and the offices of the parties bearing them
down to the level of the Afghan comprehension ; while Burnes
and others skilled in the dialect of the country, translated the
speeches as they were uttered. The Afghans are a merry people,
and have a keen relish of the ludicrous and the satirical ; and as
the interpreter never failed to bring the jokes of the actors

home to them, they marked their delight by bursting into frequent peals of laughter.

The spring begins to burst at Cabul early in March. It is not, however, genial, for the rains are heavy and incessant till about the middle of May. This is the season for snipe-shooting, which men prosecute in the intervals of the showers, looking for their game by the margin of the lake, and wherever watercourses or marshes intersect the cultivated country; and then, likewise, ducks may be followed to advantage, though they are more sought after when the ice upon the lake is strong; and the sportsman is sure to find them at the springs, which are never frozen. But, as may be supposed, both snipe and duck-shooting are followed only when the strength of the rain is interrupted, as it begins to be towards the latter part of April. Nevertheless, the officers of the British army do not appear to have wasted even the rainy season in absolute inaction. They set themselves to an employment which was exceedingly interesting in itself, and which, when the period of exhibiting its results arrived, proved to be a source of fresh wonder to their Caucasian neighbours.

The 13th Light Infantry could boast in those of a very ingenious individual among its officers. Mr. Sinclair possessed a great mechanical genius, which he now applied to the construction of a boat, which he succeeded in rendering complete in all respects during the interval of the rains. Carriages being provided, it was conveyed, with its oars, masts, and sails, to the lake, and there launched. Now there had never been seen in all Afghanistan before that moment such a thing as a boat of any description. Individual Afghans who might have strayed as far as the Indus could possibly speak on their return of the inflated hides by means of which the dwellers upon the banks of that river waft themselves from point to point; and the flying-bridges, or huge ferry-boats, which here and there cross the stream, must have had a place in their memory. But even to travellers the trim wherry in which a party of young men now embarked was entirely new, and to the multitude it became an object of astonishment indescribable. They could not comprehend the principle on which it had been fabricated. The oars, the masts, the sails, and, above all, the rudder, were marvels and mysteries to them; and when the crew, after exhibiting before them, endeavoured to explain that England possessed floating castles of the kind, capable of accommodating many hundred persons, and carrying each a hundred guns of heavy calibre, they lifted up their heads and eyes in mute amazement. It is hardly necessary to add, that of the mighty ocean it was impossible to convey to their minds any idea; for he who has not seen the sea never learns, even from books and drawings, how rightly to apprehend it; and to those who had for the first time heard of it, it was mere sound without sense.

So passed the various seasons of the year, each of which brought with it both its pleasures and its anxieties.   In winter men wrapped well up, for the thermometer at early morning was often far below zero; and the white snow upon the ground, reflecting back the rays of a sun, which moved through a sky which was almost always cloudless, tried the eyes severely, and sometimes fatally: for it is a remarkable peculiarity in the meteorological phenomena of Afghanistan, that, while the snow is falling, the blue of the heavens overhead continues as clear as ever.   In spring, out-of-door amusements were heartily entered into when the rains would permit; after which, so late as the end of June, the climate appears to have been delicious.   A clear air, with the thermometer varying from 78° to 86°, left such as breathed it free to go abroad at all hours; and encouraged them, not only to angle, as many did with great success, but to add football, hocky, and quoits to the list of their athletic sports.

Thus far all things went on as could have been desired.   The Afghan chiefs professed, and acted, as if they felt something like regard for their European invaders individually; though they never scrupled to tell them frankly, that, as a people, they were abhorred.   Moreover, excellent discipline being preserved, there occurred no grounds of collision between the occupants of the camp or the cantonments and the populace.   In one respect, however, a regard to historical truth compels us to acknowledge, that less regard was paid to the prejudices of the inhabitants than could have been wished.   Though they do not, like other Mohammedan races, universally shut up their women, the Afghans are as open to jealousy as Orientals in general, and treating their wives often rudely, the latter could not but be pleased with the attentious which the Feringhees showed them.   It is much to be feared, that our young countrymen did not always bear in mind that the domestic habits of any people ought to be sacred in the eyes of strangers.   And hence arose, by degrees, distrust, alienation, and hostility, for which it were unfair to deny that there might be some cause.   However, it is not worth while to touch upon a subject which cannot be approached without seeming to condemn where condemnation could serve no good purpose. Whatever errors they may have committed, the great mass of the garrison of Cabul atoned for them terribly ; and the survivors, as years pass over them, will doubtless more and more become convinced, that the gratification of the moment is purchased at too high a price, if it occasion deep or permanent suffering to others.

CHAPTER IX.

March of Sale's Brigade towards the Provinces—Operations at Bootkak.

THE time was now come when the return to the provinces of the regiments which the Queen's 44th and other corps had come up to relieve could no longer be deferred. The hostile movements among the villages of the Zoormut and the Ghoodabund, which had hitherto operated to postpone the arrangement, were put down ; and though rumours of the revival of a bad spirit in many quarters were rife, nobody seemed much disposed to regard them. Accordingly, in the beginning of October, 1841, Sir Robert Sale's brigade, consisting of the 13th Light Infantry, increased by drafts recently received to eight hundred bayonets, and the 35th Native Infantry, of pretty nearly the same numerical strength, was warned to be in readiness for the march. Moreover, as the march was to be conducted through provinces supposed to be peaceable, and led in a homeward direction, both corps were informed, through their commanding officers, that nothing more could possibly be exacted from them, than the good conduct which British soldiers usually display when passing from one quarter to another. The men's arms were, for the most part, of an inferior description. Old flint and steel muskets had become, through much use, so imperfect in their hands, that numbers were in the habit of missing fire continually, and the best and most serviceable in the whole brigade was just as likely to carry its ball wide of the mark as in a straight line towards it. Sir Robert Sale, who knew the importance and value of effective weapons, stated these facts at head-quarters. He reminded the authorities that there were in store four thousand muskets, constructed on the detonating principle, perfectly new, and never likely, at least with the present force, to be sullied by using ; and he begged permission to arm his regiment from that heap, and to leave his worn-out firelocks in the room of the weapons withdrawn. But General Elphinstone would not listen to the proposal. What could the 13th want with new muskets, when it was well known that, in marching out of Cabul, they were accomplishing the first stage on their journey to England? They must carry what they had with them, and they did so; of which the consequence was, that when the day of overthrow came, eight hundred serviceable muskets fell into the hands of Akbar Khan, instead of being used against him.

Though nobody seemed to apprehend that serious obstacles to the progress of the brigade would anywhere arise, still, as the means of transport were scanty, and it was found necessary to move the regiments one by one, orders were issued for the attendance upon the leading battalion of a certain amount of troops of other arms than its own. Accordingly Colonel Monteith, who with the 35th Native Infantry moved first from the cantonments, had under his orders, additional to his own corps, one hundred men of the Shah's sappers and miners, with Captain Broadfoot, of the Royal Engineers, at their head; two six-pounder guns, of which Lieut. Davis had the charge, and a squadron of the 5th regiment Bengal Light Cavalry, commanded by Captain Oldfield, of the same corps. The total amount of fighting men in this column did not probably exceed one thousand; but, as invariably happens in the East, the followers far surpassed them, and when the quantity of animals needed to transport baggage, ammunition, and hospital stores came to be computed, the extent of the line of march proved tremendous. Surely this custom of carrying a crowd of non-combatants about with our armies will, in the course of time, be set aside even in India; for it not only increases the difficulty of subsisting a force four-fold, but it interferes with the pliability of the armed body, which is usually as much concerned to save the baggage from falling into the enemy's hands as to strike a blow, or to make the dispositions which shall bring an enemy within striking distance.

Colonel Monteith set out upon his progress at an early hour on the morning of the 9th of October. He traversed that day the elevated plain which separates Cabul from the Bootkak hills, a range which, rising by degrees, connects itself with the more stupendous mountains that overhang the Koord Cabul, and after a brief interval fall in, and form a junction with, those that lie beyond. The plain in question is tolerably fertile, being washed by the waters of the Logur and the Cabul streams, which, coming down from different sources, unite about midway between the Balla Hissar and the mountains. It is open too, and the roads, though not good, are abundantly passable, at least in summer. Accordingly the march was performed without difficulty, and brought to a close in good order ; and in an open space near the village of Bootkak, having the hills on his right, and the mouth of the pass about a mile or a mile and a half before him, he pitched his tents.

Meanwhile the officers and men of the 13th Light Infantry abode quietly in their cantonments. Some of them, who had been called in from visits to their friends at a distance, expressed regret that their pleasures should have been interrupted before the time, for nobody expected that, within the compass of a week at the nearest, the rear division of the brigade would be directed to begin its journey. Wherefore the surprise of all concerned may be imagined when, about noon on the 10th, an order was suddenly issued for the regiment to pack its baggage, and set out for Bootkak at dawn on the following morning. As was to be expected, curiosity, if not a deeper feeling, everywhere awoke. Men hastened to inquire into the causes of such an unexpected change of plan ; and it can hardly be said that they received any very unlooked-for tidings when it was told them, that their comrades of the 35th had been attacked over-night, and sustained considerable loss.

The 13th were not quite prepared for moving at so short a notice. Trained and good soldiers, from the veteran to the recruit, they were ready at any moment to fight; but the means of transport available were exceedingly deficient, and the accumulation of property is always great in a corps which abides for any length of time in the same place, whether its quarters be fixed in India or in England. Hence many arrangements which individuals had intended to make were still incomplete; and even the public service, as regarded camels and other beasts of burthen, could not be supplied to the extent which the heads of departments might have wished. Nevertheless the order, sudden as it was, took no one by surprise. The men undertook cheerfully to carry their own knapsacks,—a new feature, be it observed, in Oriental warfare ; and the officers sacrificed without hesitation

every article of private baggage which it might have been inconvenient to move.   To be sure, the soldier's load was lightened to
the lowest point that seemed to be compatible with comfort.   He
was directed to pack up only one spare shirt, one pair of socks, one
pair of boots, and his blue trowsers, the whole of which, though
increased by the weight of such indispensable articles as soap,
towel, and cooking utensils, left him considerably less burthened
than an infantry soldier usually is on a home parade.   And the
more to relieve him, forty rounds of ammunition, instead of sixty,
were stowed in his pouch, the remaining twenty being carried
for him on the flank of his company by animals allotted for
this service.   Still both officers and men were put to some
inconvenience, more especially as they do not appear to have
been informed whether the morrow's march ought to be regarded
as a movement towards Hindostan, or as a mere expedition
for the relief of their comrades of the 35th.   However, no sound
of murmur, far less of complaint, was heard in their quarters.
On the contrary, they took leave of the sick of their own corps
and of such friends and intimate acquaintances as they happened
severally to possess in others, and, retiring to rest in good time,
were up, with baggage packed, and took their places in the ranks
on the first blast of the bugle.

  The 13th were excellent marchers.   They had proved themselves such both on the advance from Sukkur and in all the
various desultory operations in which they had since borne a
part ; and they swung along on the present occasion at so smart
a pace, that their sudden appearance near the camp of the 35th
excited as much of surprise as of satisfaction.   Kindly greetings
passed between the officers of the two corps, the force encamped
supplying the comers from afar with a well-earned breakfast,
after which the Europeans, pitching their own tents, made ready
for such work as their gallant leader might cut out for them
against the morrow.   Moreover, each tale that was told more
and more prepared them for hard knocks in abundance.   The
pass had, it appeared, been reconnoitred for a good way by the
Acting Quarter-Master-General, who reported that it was not
only filled with armed men, but that, at a point particularly
adapted for the arrangement, a songa, or stone barricade, had
been thrown up.   Sir Robert Sale received this statement with

characteristic coolness and good humour. He saw, from the
natural features of the country, that a few resolute men might
keep it against a thousand; and proceeded to order such arrangements as he trusted, making due allowance for the superiority of his own men over the enemy, would put the determination of its defenders to a harder trial than they should be able
to sustain.

As a step preparatory to the business of the morrow it was
necessary to provide for the security of the night. The enemy
might again come on, as they had done on a former occasion;
and Sir Robert Sale was determined that, if they did, they should
take little by their motion. With this view, strong piquets
were posted at nightfall so as to cover the camp in front, on
both flanks, and in the rear. Cavalry patrols were likewise
directed to be on the look out, particularly in the direction of
the pass and on the right; while orders were issued that, at the
first alarm, all lights should be extinguished, and regiments and
detachments assembled at their respective alarm-posts, without
beat of drum, and in profound silence. It was a wise and soldier-
like arrangement; but, either because they had had enough of it
on the night of the 10th, or that, being aware of the arrival of
European reinforcements, they considered it useless to waste
their ammunition in a repetition of the game, the enemy offered
no molestation, even to the sentries. The dark hours, therefore,
passed without disquiet; and men and baggage animals, sleeping
soundly, were refreshed.

The brigade orders of the previous evening had indicated,
with sufficient accuracy, the arrangements that were to be made
on the 12th for forcing the pass. At the first blast of the bugle,
therefore, the troops stood to their arms; and the line of march
was formed in good time, so that the whole were in readiness to
quit the ground at the hour appointed. In front of all, forming
an advanced guard, were to move two companies of the 13th.
They were to be strengthened by the two flank-companies of the
35th Native Infantry, having the guns, with Captain Broadfoot's
sappers, in immediate communication with them; while, with a
slight interval between, were to follow the two regiments, right
in front, the whole being covered by a company of the 35th as
a rear-guard. As to the camp, that was left standing, under the

protection of the guard which is usually told off for such services; and Captain Oldfield with his horsemen was enjoined
in addition to keep within the lines, not mounted, because it
was desirable that his horses should be fresh, but each man accoutred and ready to spring into the saddle on the first appearance of danger. Finally, patrols were to watch the several approaches to the camp, narrowly; and for all that might follow
they had their own good swords to trust to.

The dawn had made considerable progress, and was merging
rapidly into broad day, when, at the appointed signal, the troops
moved forward. No opposition met them till they were fairly
entangled in the pass; and then, from the rocks and precipices
on either side, such a storm of fire opened as told of itself that
the heights above were occupied in great force. So skilful, too,
were the Afghans in the art of skirmishing, that, except by the
flashes which their matchlocks emitted, it was impossible to tell
where the marksmen lay. Rocks and stones, some of them
hardly larger than a thirteen-inch shell, seemed to afford them
excellent shelter. They squatted down, showing nothing above
the crag except the long barrels of their fusils and the tops of
their turbans; and with such unerring aim were their shots
thrown, that both in the advanced guard and from the body
of the column men soon began to drop. Then might be seen
with what exceeding hardihood British soldiers throw themselves
into the teeth of danger, and, by affronting, overcome it. The
bugles sounded for the leading companies to extend, and away
among the precipices ran the skirmishers; scaling corries with
a steady foot, and returning the fire of the Afghans with great
alacrity. Meanwhile the column slackened not its pace for a
moment. Onward it pressed, detaching two or three companies
as flankers, which mounted the hills on the right and left, and
soon became warmly engaged, till by and by the stockade, or
breast-work of huge stones, wherewith the enemy had endeavoured
to block up the pass, became conspicuous. A gallant rush was
made at this work, which, however, the Afghans did not venture
to defend; and then Lieut. Davis, lashing his horses, went on
with his guns at a gallop, and at a gallop passed through.
From that time the fire of the enemy began to slacken. Their
skirmishers, indeed, had already yielded to the impetuous attack

of the leading companies, and the whole now fleeing to the crests
of the mountains, whither our men could not follow, gradually
melted away, and at last disappeared.

The loss sustained in the course of this affair was less severe
than might have been expected. Sir Robert Sale himself received a musket-ball in the ancle just as he entered the pass; and
almost at the same moment his aide-de-camp, who rode by his
side, had his horse shot under him. Captain Younghusband, of
the 35th Native Infantry, likewise, and Lieutenant Miers of the
13th, were wounded severely; and among the rank and file in
all the corps engaged casualties occurred. But the total amount
of men put *hors de combat* was wonderfully small, considering
the great advantage of position which the enemy possessed; and
of horses few were struck. Of those attached to the guns, happily
not one received damage.

The result of this successful encounter was to carry the 35th
Native Infantry, with all their baggage and followers, over one
important stage on their homeward journey. The narrowest and
most intricate portion of the pass was threaded; and in a sort of
punchbowl, or circular valley, offering a position comparatively
secure from night attacks, they made preparations for encamping.
Not so the 13th. To have left the Bootkak gorge in the hands
of the enemy would have been not only to isolate the 35th, but
to give up the communications between Cabul and the frontiers
altogether; and hence the gallant 13th had received instructions,
so soon as the barricade should be forced, to return to the camp
whence they had set out in the morning. They now proceeded
to obey these instructions; and, carrying their wounded with
them, marched back into the defile. Again they were assailed,
both from the right hand and from the left, with a desultory,
but warm skirmishing fire; and again they ran the gauntlet
through it, fighting for every inch of ground, and winning it too,
though not without some loss and considerable inconvenience.
They then returned to the tents, and to the force, mounted and
dismounted, which they had left to protect them; and slept that
night as soundly as soldiers are accustomed to do who have gone
through a sharp day's work, with honour to themselves.

G

CHAPTER X.

Night attacks on the 35th—Advance of the 13th to rejoin their comrades.

THERE was a strange delusion at this time,—a cloud, for which
it is impossible to account, upon the intellects of all the leading
functionaries in Cabul.   Nobody would believe that a terrible
revolution was at hand.   Some days previously to the march of
the 35th Native Infantry, three Ghilzie chiefs of note had suddenly quitted the capital, and the next intelligence received of
them was, that they had attacked and plundered a rich Kaffela,
or caravan, at Tizeen, and occupied, with their armed followers,
the difficult defile of Koord-Cabul.   Mohammed Akbar Khan,
likewise, the fighting son, as he was called, of Dost Mahommed,
was known to have arrived at Bameean, from Khooloom, and to
be busy, both in person and by means of his emissaries, in con-
ducting intrigues against the government.   To speak of the in-
solence both of chiefs and people in the city would be to repeat a
tale with which all Europe rang not long ago ; while far and near
about Ghuznee, not less than in Kohistan, the worst spirit was
known to prevail, without so much as a desire, as it seemed, to
hide it.   Nevertheless, Sir William Macnaghten, Sir Alexander
Burnes, and General Elphinstone, convinced, as was to be expected, by their reasoning, rejected with disdain all warnings of
danger.   There was no organised conspiracy to get rid of Shah
Shujah, or to molest his allies.   A people little used to restraint
could not be expected to submit all at once, or with a good grace,
to any settled government ; and as to attacks on Kaffelas, such
things had been from time immemorial, and could not be got rid
of for many a day ; perhaps not during the continuance of the
present generation.   To such a height, indeed, was the infatua-
tion carried, that when Sir Robert Sale communicated to head-
quarters the details of his recent march, and the results of the
operation, he received an answer of which it would be unjust to
all concerned, were it not inserted in the present narrative at

length. " The Ghilzies," so ran this memorable document, which I copy from the Orderly-Book of Sir Robert Sale's division, " are a race of hereditary robbers. Now that they have been defeated they are going about everywhere, and will, no doubt, do all the mischief they can in the dark. The remedy is this; I have sent a man to Jan Feshan Khan, desiring him to keep watch with his Jazailchies round the camp. Shir Mahmoud Khan Baboo Kuzzee should remain at the entrance of the pass at Koord Cabul; and with twenty horsemen, and one hundred footmen, guard the road to Bootkak. From Bootkak to Cabul, security of the road is committed to Meer Cotah Khan Logusee. To-morrow I will have all the caves and caverns searched, and any Ghilzie that may be found will be seized. The only favour I would beg is, that you will request the gentlemen not to move about late at night. The Major-General requests you will make the above arrangements known to the officers under your command, to prevent mistakes; but our security must, notwithstanding, depend mainly upon our own prudence and vigilance."

One clause in this remarkable despatch deserved all possible attention, namely, the last. There was no further doubt on the mind of any member of Sir Robert Sale's force, that his own safety, and that of his comrades, must henceforth depend upon the vigilance of individuals themselves; and the vigilance of videttes, sentries, piquets, and, indeed, of the troops in general, never relaxed for a moment. From day to day the brigade Orderly-Book contained this notice:—" The troops will be on the alert during the night, ready to turn out at a moment's warning;" and on the alert, clothed, accoutred, and ready for action, from the oldest to the youngest, they kept themselves. Nor, to say the truth, was the caution, either of the men or of their leaders, uncalled for. The enemy, as it afterwards came out, withdrew in a body from the pass, not relishing the idea of getting enclosed between the regiments which occupied its two extremities. Nevertheless, straggling parties of them still held to the ravines, and from time to time, especially in the night, fired from their long matchlocks into the camp. No lives. however, were lost, nor were any casualties occasioned; and in due time it came to pass, that men learned to regard such interrup-

G 2

tions with indifference, and slept on, unconcerned, so long as the voices of their own sentinels, or the notes of their own bugle, failed to rouse them.

The camp of the 13th was pitched about a couple of miles from the mouth of the pass; and a cavalry piquet posted, about a mile in advance of it, kept a good look-out, and by patrolling constantly, rendered the advance of any considerable body by stealth impossible. The patrols, moreover, were steady, and seldom brought tidings which the event failed to justify: yet once a false alarm arose, and the effect of it was to show how speedily, and with what little stir, that small but most efficient body of men could be made to turn out ready for action. One evening, after the men had lain down, and a profound silence prevailed, the noise of a horse put to his utmost speed caused the sentry to challenge. In an instant the piquet stood to its arms, and the rider being allowed to approach, and reporting that a column had been seen in the gorge, the word was passed quietly from tent to tent, and in two minutes the regiment was formed. No enemy came, however, nor was any on the way. Captain Oldfield, riding forward to reconnoitre, soon came back with intelligence that the patrol had mistaken a few of our own horsemen, bearers of a despatch, for the leading files of an Afghan division, and men and officers returned to their tents, somewhat vexed, perhaps, for the moment, at the interruption which their sleep had sustained; but more than ever satisfied that the caution which had come from head-quarters was not wasted on any member of the body.

From the 12th to the 20th of October, the 13th Light Infantry, with Captain Oldfield's squadron of the 5th Light Cavalry, occupied the encampment near Bootkak. The 35th Native Infantry, likewise, to which was added by and by a rasselah of Anderson's irregular horse, abode in their tents at Koord Cabul, both sections of the brigade being either without orders, or the orders which they received proving so vague and untelligible, that nobody felt justified in acting upon them. Meanwhile, from far and near, swarms of Ghilzies gathered to a head. Now it was reported that at Tizeen they had set up their standard; and by and by, among other rumours that spread abroad, this was stated, that the very plain in rear of Bootkak was not free from them, and that the capital itself was about to be placed in a state of siege.

It was not the business of Sir Robert Sale or his officers either to change their dispositions or to shift their ground, on account of reports which neither came to them in an official shape, nor were accompanied by any explicit instructions; but of his own immediate followers the veteran took good care. Loose stones being abundant in those parts, the piquets at their out-stations, and the several companies within the lines, were directed to throw up songas, each at its own alarm post, and to make them of a height sufficient to shelter the men while they slept, yet not so lofty as to hinder the muskets from being rested upon them, so that marksmen might take good aim from behind them as securely as under cover of a breastwork.

All this while the constituted authorities in Cabul clung with an astonishing tenacity to the persuasion that the cloud which darkened the political horizon would soon pass away. They could no longer discredit the existence of an insurrectionary movement among the hills between Jellalabad and the capital; and they seem to have admitted, though with evident reluctance, that more than a band of feudatory robbers had taken part in it. They felt, moreover, that let the cost be what it might, there was a necessity for re-establishing their communications with the provinces, which the insurgents had cut off. Hence reinforcements of all arms were marched to join Sir Robert Sale; so that there arrived between the 13th and 18th, first, two guns of European horse-artillery, under Lieutenant Walker; next four companies of the 37th Native Infantry; and, by and by, Captain Backhouse's mountain train; three hundred additional sappers; Captain Abbott's battery, fresh from service in the Zoormut valley; and the remaining companies of the 37th. And high time it was that Sale's corps should be strengthened and rendered serviceable; for the 35th had again been attacked in their position; and the Afghan horsemen who served with them proving treacherous, the enemy had penetrated unchallenged within their lines, and caused a severe loss, both in killed and wounded, ere they were driven off.

Not without some foretaste of the difficulties which awaited them had these reinforcements reached the point on which they were directed. By some strange mismanagement a detachment of artillery was sent from Cabul without an escort; and the consequence was that though the troopers and their guns, and the tumbrils attached to them, arrived safely in camp, their baggage, animals, and followers were attacked, and the whole of the horses' clothing, as well as the men's tents, carried off. Both men and horses suffered from this loss; nevertheless they were ready, and in excellent humour, for whatever services might be required of them; and on the morning of the 20th the forward movement began. It was uninterrupted in any way till they reached Khoord Cabul. The necessity to which the men were subjected of repeatedly fording a stream which runs through the gorge, and came with its waters more than half-leg high, proved disagreeable enough; for the season was now considerably advanced, and at night the cold began to be severe. But beyond this no inconvenience befel them. Not an enemy appeared; and the baggage keeping well up, and the horses and camels sustaining their loads stoutly, the whole arrived in excellent order and without loss, long before noon, at the camp of their comrades.

The sick and wounded of the 13th had been sent back to Cabul previously to this advance. Those from the 35th were met midway in the pass, journeying in the same direction, and they amounted to eighty persons; for the night affair of the 27th had been a sharp one. Treason co-operated with open violence to work the regiment wrong, It appeared that about noon on the 17th Captain Mac Gregor, the political agent for Jellalabad, who accompanied the 35th, received a written communication from a chief at Kubber Jubber, which announced that the writer "was two hours' march from the British camp, and intended to attack it, against a specified time." An answer was sent back in the same spirit of familiarity, whereby the Kubber chief was advised to make haste, otherwise he might find himself too late for the fun; and the regiment made such preparations as were judged necessary. But no provision could be made against the coming in of a body of Doorannees, who, having heretofore been regarded as among the most loyal of Shah Shujah's subjects, were permitted to pitch their tents close to that of the political agent. Nothing occurred, however, till about 9 o'clock, when, as the troops stood to their arms, tidings were brought that a strong column was advancing on the rear of the camp. The grenadier company immediately faced about, and moved towards the point threatened ; but they had just cleared the place where the commissariat camels were picketed, when a large body of armed men sprang up from behind the beasts of burden, and fired upon them. Thirty Sipahis, with Captain Jenkins their leader, fell, and the friendly Afghans made a rush towards the baggage : for the people who had joined them late in the afternoon were those from whom this damage came ; and the confusion caused by the discovery that the camp was full of traitors, proved, for the moment, considerable. Discipline and courage are not, however, under any circumstances, to be taken quite by surprise. The gallant 35th soon extricated themselves from this dilemma, and took ample vengeance upon the robbers ; while the chief from Kubber Jubber, after giving and receiving a few pretty close discharges, retired. That night cost Sir Robert Sale's brigade some valuable lives ; and when an account was taken of the camels on the morrow, not fewer than eighty, including one laden with ammunition, were found to be missing.

For the loss of baggage animals to a force circumstanced as was this, nothing could compensate. Application had been made to get the deficiency supplied from the capital ; but not a hoof came, and Sir Robert Sale determined, let the consequences be what they might, that he should not budge an inch from his present position till they did come. He therefore turned a deaf ear to the suggestion that it would be both practicable and convenient to push by divisions upon Jellalabad. He had seen enough of the state of the country to convince him that there could be no more passing through it except by dint of hard fighting ; and he was too good a soldier to think of exposing his brigade to be cut to pieces in detail. Steadily, therefore, he persisted in his determination not to penetrate beyond Koord Cabul till he should be enabled to do so in force ; and his firmness prevailed. On the evening of the 21st such a supply of camels arrived as would suffice to carry the whole of the baggage, including tents, hospital stores, and ammunition ; and orders were issued the same hour, that the advance should be begun at an early hour on the morrow.

CHAPTER XI.

March to Tizeen—Affair in the Valley.

It was still dark on the morning of the 22nd of October, when a general stir in the camp began. Bat-men saddled their horses; camel-drivers and the keepers of Yaboos or ponies got the animals ready; and ammunition-boxes, arm-chests, bags of provision, and other necessaries, were conveyed to their proper stations. By and by came the striking and rolling of tents; and finally, the strapping of all these, with officers' trunks, and the little extra baggage that accompanied the force, on the backs of the beasts of burden. Meanwhile, after snatching a hasty meal, the Europeans a morsel of bread, and a cup of coffee, or a glass of rum and water; the Hindostanees their otta or boiled rice; the line of march was formed. The advanced guard was composed of six companies of infantry, two being furnished from each corps, those from the 13th leading. They were supported by two 9-pounders and the mountain train, the latter consisting of 3-pounders, which, though now horsed in the ordinary way, used to be taken to pieces and conveyed on the backs of camels— as the Duke of Wellington conveyed the lightest of his artillery on the backs of mules over the more rugged of the passes of the Pyrenees. Three companies of sappers moved in rear of the guns, having a troop of the 5th Light Cavalry to cover them; and the whole were commanded by Lieutenant-Colonel Monteith, of the 35th Native Infantry.

Such was the advanced guard—a strong force, though certainly not stronger than the nature of the country demanded. The main column, consisting of the three infantry regiments, with Abbott's battery, was led by Colonel Dennie, inasmuch as Sir Robert Sale's wound still incapacitated him from taking his proper place in the field; while the rear guard, composed of some Afghan riflemen, with Anderson's horse, and the remaining troop of the 5th Cavalry, acted under the orders of Captain

Oldfield.   With respect to the baggage, it was directed to move
between the tail of the column and the head of the rear-guard;
and the road being narrow it occupied a space so extended as to
separate the latter from the former of these armed bodies somewhat inconveniently.

It was about seven o'clock in the morning, when, all things
being pronounced to be in order, the word was given to march.
Not a bugle sounded, nor was a drum beaten; but with a measured tread, and having their nerves wound up to a pitch of high
excitement, the little army quitted its ground.   Two files of the
13th led the way; then followed, with a slight interval between,
a subdivision of the same corps; and by and by, after a second
interval, the head of the advanced guard.   For a brief space—
that is, while yet they traversed the valley or punch-bowl—Colonel Monteith had his flankers out.   But the valley soon came
to an end; and with rocks rising shere and perpendicular, on
either side of the narrow way into which it sank, their services
ceased to be available.   They were therefore called in, and moved
on in their proper places, with their comrades.   It is hardly necessary to state that troops passing through such a ravine as that
into which Sale's brigade had now plunged, however brave and
disciplined they may be, feel that they are powerless.   They look
to the right hand and to the left, and behold that a wall shuts them
in.   They see that to change their formation is impossible; and
that a few resolute men—indeed, that women, or even children,
might, by rolling huge stones over the precipices, destroy them.
Happily for Sale's brigade, not an enemy appeared upon the tops
of the nearer ridges throughout the whole of a seventeen miles'
march.   On some of the more distant peaks which overtopped
the precipitous edges of the ravine, horsemen here and there
showed themselves; and as the advanced companies drew towards
Kubber Jubber, the word was passed to be upon the alert.   But
even Kubber Jubber, though well adapted, from the nature of
the ground, for a resolute stand, was abandoned, and the whole
column, including both the baggage and the rear-guard, passed
it unmolested.

For seventeen miles or thereabouts the column wound its way
through this terrific and circuitous pass; and at last saw before
it the opening of the valley of Tizeen.   This is one of those

natural hollows which occur at intervals among all the mountain
ranges of Afghanistan, forming, as it were, halting-places for
caravans, because of the herbage wherewith they are partially
covered. A fort or tower stands on the slope of one of the
mountains, which recede from each other to a distance of perhaps five English miles; and hamlets scattered here and there
give shelter to the tribe which pays obedience to the chief who
inhabits it. The valley of Tizeen would be picturesque in the
extreme if there were any natural wood to adorn it; but except
a few fruit-trees planted about the chieftain's castle, not a leaf
is to be seen from one extremity to the other. Nevertheless, the
softened character of the hills, which here lay aside in part their
rugged formations, gives relief to the eye, as well as to the ima-
gination, which has grown weary by this time of dealing entirely
with the terrific, and longs to have associations stirred that connect themselves with pastoral rather than with robber life. For
stern in the extreme were all the associations which in the course
of their progress heretofore had been stirred in these hardy
soldiers. Black, bald, and barren rocks closing in and hanging
over them continually, without a shrub, or tree, or blade of
grass to ornament them, had fatigued both the mind and the
vision; and now the men felt positively glad at the prospect of
passing for awhile through a gentler country.

You do not come upon the valley of Tizeen all at once. The
pass widens a little as you approach two huge rocks, which, pushing out their shoulders on the right hand and on the left, look
like two huge door-posts on which a pair of enormous folding
gates might be swung. The leading files were already between
these rocks, when the officer commanding saw, just inside their
curvature, a small body of Afghan horse drawn up. He halted
his men, and riding back in all haste, suggested to Colonel
Monteith that it would be a good thing to let loose the cavalry
upon them, inasmuch as they might easily be cut off. Colonel
Monteith, however, was too prudent a soldier to throw his
people in such a country by driblets out of hand; so he closed
up the whole of the advanced guard, and moved forward. It
was well that he did so. No sooner were the projecting crags
turned than the hills which bounded the valley on all sides were
seen to swarm with Afghans, who had manifestly placed this

body of horse as a decoy wherewith to entice the British cavalry forward, and to bring them under such a fire as must have emptied every saddle in a moment. Now then was the time to act ; and Colonel Monteith did not suffer the fortunate moment to escape him.

The guns were immediately ordered to the front. They came up at a hand-gallop, the infantry opening to the right and left in order to let them pass; and unlimbering with all haste, the artillerymen threw some shells with admirable precision among the masses; the effect was very striking. You saw some men fall, and the rest, as if terrified at finding themselves in so exposed a situation, waved to and fro, and then broke, and retired in all directions. At this moment Colonel Dennie rode up ; and a gallant young officer of the 13th, Lieutenant E. King* by name, eagerly entreated that he might have leave, with the company which he commanded, to drive " the rascals," as he termed them, from the hill to which they had retreated. Dennie threw a rapid glance over the scene, and, to the great delight of Mr. King, replied " Surely." Both companies of the 13th formed, and forward they went, one led by Mr. King, the other by Lieut. Rattray, of the same regiment, at the double step, and in skirmishing order.

The affair that followed resembled for a while rather the pursuit of a defeated enemy than an attack upon a strong position. There was a good deal of firing on both sides, but the Afghans made no stand. They retreated with great celerity, each man as he delivered his shot, till the whole were fairly pushed over the hill, and were seen ascending another that lay beyond it. It would have been well for the brave fellows who had carried this nearer height had they been content with their first success. No good was to be gained by crossing the dell that lay under it ; for the Afghans could not from the ground to which they had withdrawn molest the column on its march, and nothing more was needed or desired than to keep open the road along which the column moved. But young soldiers, like hunters imperfectly broken to their work, are apt to be carried away by the excitement of success ; and seeing the enemy halt, turn round, and begin to throw long

* This was he who made himself so conspicuous for his bravery at the assault on the castle of Julgah.

shots at them across the valley, our people set up a shout, and
dashed forward. The skirmish was warmer, and the ground better
contested on this occasion, than before. The hill, indeed, was
steeper, and the Afghans, though they rarely permitted our men
to come within three hundred yards of them, kept up a warm fire
from behind the many rocks and crags with which its face was
broken. But they could not maintain their ground. They were
forced back and back, till they began to disappear over the
ridge; whereupon the assailants, whose last move had not been approved of by Colonel Dennie, were at length, though not without
some difficulty, halted.

Colonel Dennie had seen from his post upon the road that his
fiery young friends were getting into a scrape. He therefore
ordered up two additional companies, with a body of the Shah's
sappers, to reinforce them; and these troops did their duty well,
and took their own share in the later skirmish. They sustained
some loss likewise; for Lieut. Orr, a good officer, who commanded
the sappers, was severely wounded on the very crest of the hill;
a private of the 13th falling dead at the same moment beside
him. The whole, however, halted at last; and till four o'clock
in the afternoon kept their ground, which was by no means
favourable, against repeated though desultory advances by the
enemy. Meanwhile the main body of the division moved on
unmolested; but just as the baggage approached the termination
of the pass, a warm fire opened upon it and upon the rear-guard
from the hills that hung over them. A considerable loss and
great confusion was the consequence. Many camp-followers
fled, leaving the camels and other beasts of burthen to their fate.
The cavalry could offer no resistance to marksmen perched upon
the sides of overhanging rocks, and the Shah's riflemen seemed
scarcely in earnest in their efforts to dislodge them. Now it was
in operations such as this that, from the beginning to the end of
the war, the Afghans proved themselves to be especially skilful.
Though individually brave, they seldom stood to oppose our men
either in a stand-up fight upon the plain, or in a smart skirmish:
but wherever they found an opening whereby to approach our
baggage and rear-guards at a disadvantage, no troops in the
world knew better how to turn it to account. They slew this day
a good many men, and carried off no inconsiderable portion of

booty ; of which it would be hard to say whether our people grudged them the most nine new hospital tents, which with all the furniture they appropriated, or certain kegs containing not fewer than thirty thousand rounds of musket ammunition.

While the main body thus pushed on, and the rear sustained loss and damage, the skirmishers who covered the line of march from the hill which they had so gallantly carried, were becoming every hour environed by dangers, more formidable than they seem to have anticipated when the morning's work began. Their ammunition grew short, insomuch that they ceased by degrees to reply to the fire of the enemy, and failed therefore to keep them at a distance. At this unlucky moment likewise, an order, which they do not appear rightly to have understood, arrived to direct them in their retreat. The instructions issued were, that they should withdraw by alternate companies, one descending the hill and passing over to the nearer height, while the other, holding its ground, should keep the Afghans at bay. But either because the message was delivered indistinctly, or that they all felt themselves to be alike useless with empty pouches, the whole force, as soon as the movement was supposed to be sanctioned, began their retreat together. Moreover it soon became, as retreats conducted under similar circumstances invariably do, little better than a race. Away the men ran helter-skelter down the declivity, while the enemy, taking courage from the panic which they believed to have fallen upon the Feringhees, followed close upon their heels. It was to no purpose that Lieutenants Rattray and King called aloud to the men to slacken their pace, or warned them that the Afghans were closing upon them. They neither paused to show a front, nor took the smallest pains to keep themselves under cover, but rushed down the descent and over the glen, and reached the opposite rise eagerly. Meanwhile the officers, gathering some eight or ten men about them, took post behind a range of low rocks, and made a show of resistance : but when the enemy were arrived within twenty yards of the position, the men declared, with one accord, that they had not a cartridge left ; and, no longer restrained by the voices of the officers, took to their heels. It was a run for life or death on all sides, and not in all quarters conducted successfully. Lieut. Rattray escaped,

his safety being occasioned by a fall from a rock, which might
have killed him, but which merely carried him, at the expense
of a few bruises, out of the range of the shot, which sang round
him like hail.   Lieut. King was not so fortunate; an Afghan
bullet pierced his heart, and he rolled dead to the bottom of the
declivity.   He was a gallant and chivalrous young soldier, whom
his comrades greatly loved, and over whose untimely fate they
mourned with much sincerity.   Yet he died a soldier's death ;
and now that time has in some measure closed up the wound in
their spirits, both his relatives and they who saw him fall cannot
but find comfort in this remembrance of him.

Having cleared the ravine which separated the two hills, the
skirmishers, supplied with fresh ammunition, and reinforced by
three more companies, took up their ground on that which they
had first won.   It was called the Tower-hill, because of the
chief's castle which crowned one of its lower ridges, and formed a
better position for protecting the army on its march than that to
which their impetuosity had carried them.   They were repeatedly threatened, but never seriously attacked ; for the manner in
which they saluted the more daring of their assailants proved
that they had made up their minds not to be driven off ; and the
valour of the enemy seldom led them to seek, by hard fighting,
any object which our troops appeared determined not to surrender on other terms.   Moreover, just before dark, Abbott's
guns opened with shot and shell upon the masses which
threatened them, and they soon melted away.   Having remained,
therefore, on the rising ground till ten or eleven o'clock at
night, the flankers were recalled by orders from Sir Robert Sale,
and marched into camp.

CHAPTER XII.

March from Tizeen—Rear-guard engaged.

THE same caution which had marked the whole of Sir Robert Sale's proceedings from the outset was manifested in the arrangement of his camp in the valley of Tizeen. Strong piquets were planted on every side, and not they alone, but the advanced sentries were ordered to construct songas for their own protection; while within the lines breastworks of loose stones were thrown up, from behind which the troops might be able to defend themselves against a large superiority of numbers. Not contented with these precautions, Sir Robert made arrangements for attacking, on the morrow, the chief's castle; and one-half the amount of his infantry, together with a still larger proportion of his artillery, were directed to follow Col. Dennie on this service. But just as the troops had paraded, and were preparing to quit the ground, a messenger came in from the obnoxious chief with a letter to the political agent, in which he professed his inability to resist the Feringhees, and proposed to come to an accommodation with them. " I know," so ran his despatch, " that I and my countrymen cannot pretend to cope with your soldiers. If, therefore, you attack my castle, I shall flee to the hills, destroying, before I go, my whole stock of provisions for the winter. We may starve, but you will not be benefited; and starving men sometimes do desperate things. I do not wish to fight any more; offer me terms."

Captain MacGregor, having read this characteristic communication, proceeded with it to General Sale's tent; and expressing an opinion that the writer would cheerfully agree to such conditions as might be proposed, he prevailed upon the General to counter-order the march of the troops that had been about to operate against the tower. Neither, as it seemed, had the political agent suffered his hopes to outrun probabilities; for the chief of Tizeen expressed his willingness to come into the treaty

proposed, and to give hostages for his faithful fulfilment of it.
Accordingly about six o'clock in the evening of the 23rd, ten
heads of families arrived in the camp, who were placed under
surveillance rather for appearance's sake than because of any
use that would be made of them ; for the slaughter of hostages is
an atrocity unknown with English armies, whether serving in the
East or in the West. However, it was taken for granted that the
Afghans could not possibly be aware of this difference between
their usages and ours : and the presence among them of these ten
poor wretches, who looked more like the outcasts of a tribe
than its leading members, induced the inhabitants of the British
camp to hope for an immediate pacification of the valley.

Thus far the chief was true to his word, that, in the course of
the 25th, considerable supplies of provisions and forage were
sent into camp.   The people who brought them, however, seemed
to be excessively out of humour, and would neither accept nor
bestow the smallest civilities on the strangers ; indeed, it was observed by more than one of our people, that when they went away
they spat on the ground—a sure token of their contempt and abhorrence of the parties with which they had just been conversing.
The consequence was, that strict orders were issued to hinder
either soldiers or followers from wandering beyond the line of
the advanced sentries, while severe punishment was denounced
against such as might be convicted of plundering any of the
villages, or solitary huts, that were scattered through the valley.
In like manner the camels were prohibited from being led to
pasture far across the plain ; and wherever they went, it was directed that a guard should attend them ; "Though the enemy
have given hostages," ran one of Sir Robert Sale's orders, "it
would be both imprudent and unsafe in us to relax our vigilance.
The troops will therefore sleep fully accoutred, in front of their
lines, and under cover of the breastworks ; and the piquets and
sentries will be as much as ever upon the alert, knowing that on
our own vigilance both our honour and our safety depend."

In the course of the 23rd, an attempt was made to recover
part of the baggage which had been left in the pass, by sending
back two companies of Native Infantry to look for it.   The
search was not very profitable in any respect, and especially
failed in regard to a point which was felt at this moment to be

more important than any other. None of the camels or horses
which had broken loose amid the confusion were found; and the
loss, as well in this way, as by death, whether through over-
fatigue or by the bullets of the enemy, had become so great as
seriously to affect the pliability of the division. Indeed, so deficient did he find himself in the means of transport, that Sir
Robert Sale, when the time came for moving on, determined to
move with no more than his original command. Accordingly
the 37th Native Infantry, with a detachment from Captain Backhouse's mountain train, and three companies of sappers under
a European officer, were directed to stand fast, the Deputy
Assistant Quarter Master General being instructed to make
choice for them of a defensible position; and to await in the
valley of Tizeen the coming up of the 54th, which the General
had been led to believe would arrive in a few days, bringing
with it a convoy of sick on the way to the provinces, and some
treasure for the use of his own brigade. As soon as these should
arrive, the 37th were to conduct both sick and treasure to Jellalabad, and, whether they came early or late, Major Griffiths,
commanding the 37th, was requested to communicate as frequently
as possible with Sir Robert Sale and the rest of the division.

Having adjusted these matters, and appropriated to his own
use every disposable animal that seemed capable of bearing a
burthen, General Sale gave orders that at half-past six on the
morning of the 26th, the column of march should be formed.
The troops were to fall in right in front, having for the advanced
guard two companies of the 13th Light Infantry, four guns of
Captain Abbott's battery, two companies 35th Native Infantry,
and one company of Sappers; the main body was to consist of
the strength of the two regiments; and to be followed, first by
the ammunition and ordnance stores, under the escort of a company of Sappers, and next by Captain Backhouse's mountain-
train, that is to say, by as many guns as had not been allotted for
the strengthening of the position of the 37th regiment. Next
moved the baggage, a long and cumbrous line, the charge of
which was devolved upon a troop of the 5th Light Cavalry, and
a rasselah of the Shah's horse; with instructions to distribute themselves as much as possible along either flank, so as to
afford protection from marauders to this by far the feeblest

H

portion of the cavalcade. Finally, a strong rear-guard, consisting
of two guns from Abbott's battery, two companies of the 35th
Native Infantry, one company of Sappers, and the remaining
troop of the 5th Light Cavalry, closed the column, and acted
under the orders of Captain Oldfield, an officer of much intelligence, and unconquerable courage and activity.

Little occurred in the course of the march of the 26th of which
it is necessary to make mention. The route of the column lay
through a country less difficult than that which it had already
passed; yet so commanded at every step as to render extreme vigilance on the part of the officers necessary; but it did so happen
that not on any occasion were the advanced parties withstood, or
the progress of the main body interrupted. The rear-guard, to
be sure, was exposed as usual to a good deal of desultory fighting. It produced, however, few casualties, and, thanks to the
excellent arrangements that had been made, occasioned neither
loss nor confusion among their baggage. So that, after compass-
ing about ten English miles, the whole arrived in good order at
a place called Seh-Baba, where the tents were pitched.

To explain how the camp was arranged and protected from
one night to another; how the outposts were stationed, and the
sentries covered; and the troops within the lines sent to rest
armed and accoutred, would be to repeat a tale which, in its re-
iteration, however interesting when first told, could not fail to
weary both the reader and the writer. Enough is done when I
state, that no precaution required by the critical position of
the force was omitted to ensure its safety; and that care was
taken not only to issue provisions regularly, but to see that they
were carefully cooked and eaten. In spite, therefore, of fatigue
and much watching, the brigade enjoyed as good health as the
veteran officer at its head could have wished; for the return of
sick, which now lies before me, presents a list of little else than
of gallant fellows, officers and privates, who had received wounds
in the course of their encounters with the enemy.

Having reached the ground in good time on the 26th, the
troops were enabled to make themselves comfortable; and an
opportunity was afforded to the Brigadier of circulating among
the several corps copies of the general orders which overtook
him on the march to Cabul. These related principally to the

distribution of the force which was to remain in Afghanistan, and were only so far of interest to Sale's brigade, that they explained what was already understood, and had been acted upon from the outset; namely, that the 13th and 35th regiments were on their march to the provinces, and that the 37th had been directed to join them. But the 37th Sale had already ordered back as far as Kubber Jubber, partly because the valley of Tizeen was considered too exposed, partly in order that they might be nearer to a supply of baggage animals, without receiving which their movement on Jellalabad had become impracticable. Accordingly, though men read and made their remarks on the probable results as these might affect the convenience and comforts of others, their thoughts soon reverted to a consideration of their own position, which the progress of each new hour more and more tended to convince them was beset with grave difficulties, and surrounded with very many dangers.

At the usual hour in the morning of the 28th the march of the brigade began. It was conducted in the same order as before; but partly because the country became more difficult as the troops advanced, partly because the absence of serious molestation throughout the preceding day led the camp followers to relax in their discipline during the present, a greater disposition to stray from beneath the protection of the column was exhibited than proved either judicious or safe. The road ran to-day through a sort of broken valley, hemmed in as usual by precipitous rocks; but having some width in itself, though interrupted continually by bold hills or heights that reared themselves at intervals throughout its whole extent. A winding course was therefore that which the troops followed; and they ascended and descended continually short, steep hills, after traversing one of which all the length of way which might have been previously compassed was hidden from view. On the right hand and on the left, likewise, similar waves of rock and soil were rolled; so that the straggler who ventured perhaps a hundred yards from the flank of the column disappeared altogether. Such a country, with its ribs of granite closing in the whole, offers far greater facilities of attack to an active enemy than a mere gorge hemmed in between two walls. Walls of rock are for the most part as precipitous, and therefore as inac-

H 2

cessible from the rear as from the front; or else they furnish no
cover to marksmen who surmount them; and not unfrequently,
by receding towards their ridges, hinder such as may have ascended thither from obtaining any view of the road that passes
beneath.   But dips and hollows, such as the brigade this day
encountered, seem made for affording cover to ambuscades and
plunderers ; and both were encountered abundantly as the march
proceeded.

It was not the custom of the Afghans to measure themselves
with our troops so long as there seemed to be any chance of
acquiring spoil without it; and to-day both the advanced guard
and the main body held their course unmolested.   But no sooner
had the head of the line of baggage passed a certain point than
the business of plunder began.   An unfortunate grass-cutter,
having wandered but a few yards apart from the baggage-
guard, was set upon by a band of men who lay hidden behind
some rocks, and murdered.   This done, the assassins opened
a fire upon the camels and their leaders, which was taken up
far and near by clouds of their companions; and by and by the
faces of the far-off hills were seen to swarm with armed men.
It would not do to halt the column for such an interruption as
this.   Where an object is to be gained in war, the officer who
commands must disregard as much as possible minor inconve-
niences, and press steadily toward the end ; and Sir Robert Sale,
acting upon this principle, caused his little army to continue its
march as it had heretofore done.   But he detached company
after company from the column, throwing one upon this height
and another upon that ; and so distributing the whole that they
should furnish a succession of guards to the baggage and the
camp-followers at every point along the road which seemed
more than others to require protection.   By these means the
enemy's attention was turned from those who could not defend
themselves; and they were forced, instead of killing camels and
ponies, to enter upon a series of warm skirmishes, from which,
if our people sustained some loss, the loss caused to the aggres-
sors was much greater.

This state of things continued throughout the whole of the
day's march, and came to an end only when, at a place called
Kutta Sing, the troops halted.   Neither after the tents were

pitched did the enemy venture to approach, for they appear by
this time to have been taught that a British camp is not like an
Afghan outspan, a mere mass of human beings in confusion.
But multitudes were seen by the piquets crossing the road all
night long, as if there were some great design in progress, and
armed men were concentrating in order to effect it. The political agent being informed of all this received the announcement with perfect indifference. He assured Sir Robert Sale that
there was no national feeling of hostility towards the English
anywhere. The brigade was now in the most savage part of the
kingdom, where every chief was a leader of brigands and every
man a robber : but after the arrangements that had been entered
into with the Tizeen Patriarch, it was not to be thought of that
any opposition would be made to its onward progress. All,
therefore, that was necessary seemed to be, that the rear and the
baggage should be looked to ; for he had reason to believe that
sixty or eighty ruffians had combined to harass the morrow's
march, and it would be well to keep an eye to them from the first.

Thus warned, and looking perhaps rather to his own anticipa-
tions of what might befal than to Captain MacGregor's assurances,
Sir Robert Sale issued in the course of the day fresh and strin-
gent orders relative to the disposition of the march on the morrow. He directed Lieut. Meyne, with a detachment of cavalry,
to be on the alert at the sounding of the first bugle, and to stop
and turn back any camp followers who might endeavour, as
many of them seemed inclined, to precede the brigade in its
advance. Similar instructions were given to the officers in command of the piquets by which the flanks of the camp were
covered. On no account whatever could man or beast be suffered to obstruct the road, or to pass beyond his legitimate place
in the line of march ; for the safety of the whole depended on
the freedom and readiness with which corps and armed bodies
should be able to form up and act in case of danger. For the
same reason, and to prevent any loss or confusion in the event
of an attack, quarter-masters of regiments were informed that
the proper place for their spare ammunition was on the right
flank of their respective corps, and they were charged to have
their animals loaded and led to their stations in good time. No
particle of baggage, whether public or private, was to move

with the magazines; and even the sick, with the hospital tents and stores, had a place assigned to them, guarded indeed, and therefore comparatively safe, yet clear of all risk of interference with the formations of the fighting part of the force. Finally, the men were to sleep accoutred, while the companies appointed to act as a rear-guard next day were directed to relieve the outposts after sunset, so that they might be on their ground, and afford adequate protection to the camp as soon as it should begin to move.

It was well for the brigade that the General had taken a more serious view of the state of affairs than the political agent; for the column had scarcely quitted its ground, and the baggage was yet halted, when not sixty or eighty, but some hundreds of well-armed men, rose from behind the hillocks and broken ground that lay about the camp, and fell fiercely upon the rear-guard. The firing on both sides was warm and incessant; and though Backhouse's mountain guns sent showers of grape and shrapnell among the assailants, they were not to be denied. Men began to drop, few killed but many wounded; and the difficulty of conveying them away, through the absence of a sufficient number of doolies, became constantly greater. Not one, however, was left behind. The rear-guard fought stoutly: they never yielded a foot of ground till all behind them was clear and at a sufficient distance; and even then they merely passed from one favourable position to another, where they might again make a stand. So the greater portion of the day was spent; for the enemy, though they did not succeed in picking up a single camel, hung upon the line of march till it drew to an end: and when the list of casualties came to be taken, which was done as soon after the pitching of the tents as possible, it showed a considerable addition to the number of helpless persons, in which list Lieut. Jennings, of the 13th, having received a severe wound through the arm, was included.

CHAPTER XIII.

March to Gundamuck—Smart Affair with the Rear-guard.

THUS far the progress of the little army had been conducted without much loss or any great pressure from fatigue. The marches were generally short: that of the 28th of October hardly exceeded five miles; and though the road was rough, from the quantity of loose stones which covered it, and therefore exceedingly inconvenient for wheel-carriages, both men and horses managed to get along without foundering. The greatest trial of all was the want of forage. Not a blade of grass grew, except here and there, and in very small patches, along the entire course of the glen; and the water was in some places so impregnated with mineral substances, that neither men nor animals could drink it. The cold, likewise, after sunset, became doubly sharp in consequence of the great heat of the day, and all were exposed to it; for it was only when a halt of a day or two had been determined upon, that the tents were pitched. No body of troops could, however, preserve better order or sustain a nobler spirit. Crime was unknown: nobody marauded; nobody indulged to excess in the use of spirituous liquors; and the consequence was that at every hour, both of the day and night, the whole (from the general down to the drum-boy) were ready and willing to undertake any service.

The division was now approaching a part of the road, after crossing which, provided it were done well, an opinion prevailed, both in camp and elsewhere, that the main obstacle to their safe arrival at Jellalabad would be surmounted. How it might fare with them amid the descent of the Khyber, nobody appeared to know; but supposing them to be fairly clear of the pass of Jugdulluck, and to reach the cantonments of Gundamuck, then there was nothing more to stop them in their progress towards the town, where rest would be afforded them. Moreover, by following the more circuitous of the two roads which lead from

Tizeen to the valley of Jugdulluck, they had thrown the hostile
natives considerably out in their calculations. As it came afterwards to be known, the Ooloos (for this tribe it is which inhabits
the mountain-ranges from Seh Baba to the extreme verge of
the Gundamuck valley) had counted on the advance of the Feringhees through the Peri pass, and had, in consequence, not only
fortified it midway, but had drawn thither every disposable
man, with the intention of fighting a great battle. But Sir
Robert Sale, suspecting the intention, had wisely diverged from
this gorge, and determined to face, and by dint of hard fighting,
if necessary, to force the ravine into Jugdulluck. At the same
time, the continued movement of clouds of men during the
afternoon of the 28th, and, indeed, all night long, round the
camp and away towards the pass in question, left no room to
doubt that there would be hard work for both parties ere the
valley that lay beyond it could be reached. Not on this account,
however, was any change of plan, much less of route, contemplated ;
on the contrary, the troops were warned that the march would
begin at the usual hour, half-past seven, on the following morning, care being taken to reinforce considerably both the advanced
guard and the rear-guard ; and to support them with a stronger
artillery than as yet had been allotted to this service—the former
having four guns from Abbott's battery attached, the latter two
from the same effective corps.

The road on which the division now entered runs for several
miles along the bottom of a narrow mountain defile.   It is
hemmed in on both sides. not like the path between Bootkak and
Jubber Kubber, by perpendicular cliffs, but by a succession of
mountains, one rising above the other till the whole are terminated far in the rear by a long line of sugar-loaf granite peaks.
These hills, though both steep and stony, are quite accessible
by active men, and approach so close to the road, that marksmen
firing from the summits of the nearest, may do execution upon
a column beneath, though their aim will of course be uncertain.
Moreover, here and there in the face of this range gullies and
ravines show themselves, which communicate with other valleys
behind the range, and are used by the inhabitants as the ordinary
channels of communication with them.   Such a pass the military
reader will at once perceive presented obstacles to the march of

troops a thousandfold more formidable than any mere rent, so to speak, through the heart of a chain of rocks ; and Sir Robert Sale, who was neither ignorant of the locality nor inclined to underrate its importance, made his dispositions for a battle, should it be forced upon him, with characteristic energy and self-possession.

The usual distribution of the force into advance, main body, and rear-guard, was of course made ; and the companies allotted for the latter service being ordered upon piquet at sunset, were in their places and ready to cover the march of the baggage after the column had moved on. Protection, however, was required this day for the column itself, as well as for the baggage, and flanking parties were in consequence thrown out to clear the nearest hills. These soon became engaged in a very lively skirmish, for the enemy crowded the face of the ascent, and showed themselves not less skilful than heretofore in taking advantage of every cover that offered. Nevertheless, our men pressed on, and reinforcements being from time to time sent to them, they gained ground upon the Afghans, though not without sustaining some loss. Among the light troops who distinguished themselves on that occasion, it is but justice to particularise two companies of Goorkhas, forming a portion of that corps of the Shah Shujah's army which accompanied Sir Robert Sale's column. Small men, but resolute and active, they ran from rock to rock with surprising celerity, and delivered their fire with a degree of accuracy and a correctness of aim which won for them the applause of their European comrades. The officers and men of the 13th, though excellent skirmishers themselves, beheld the working of these wild mountaineers with delight.

Up and up the mountain-side the light troops scrambled, till they attained the summits of the nearest spurs, and looked down upon the column winding beneath, at a distance of full two thousand feet. The rarefaction of the atmosphere at this great altitude (for the road in the pass was full five thousand feet above the level of the sea) combined with the intense heat to blow the men exceedingly : so the bugles sounded a halt, and all lay down to refresh. Unfortunately, however, the halt took place on the left of the line of march, just within long range of a breast-work ; from behind which, on the slope of another hill, a party

of the enemy kept up an incessant fusilade.   One officer, Lieutenant Rattray, of the 13th, and several men, were wounded on
that occasion ; and more might have suffered, had not the bugles
from below warned the skirmishers to move on.   They did so,
holding the high grounds which they had won, and sweeping
from before them clouds of the enemy, who forthwith betook
themselves to the more remote ridges.   But, however efficacious
the proceeding might be in covering the head, and indeed the
whole extent of the column, from insult, it left the rear-guard
exposed to serious dangers, which were not slow in showing
themselves.   The enemy, though beaten from the nearer hills,
were not cowed.   On the contrary, they retired into the valley
on the other side ; and, passing round, came out at the different
ravines of which notice has been taken as falling in upon the road
at various points near the beginning of the pass.   Their numbers
were very formidable ; and whether because the sense of a decided superiority in this respect gave them courage, or that the
string of camels and ponies that passed under their view inflamed
their cupidity, they rushed into action against the rear-guard
with a degree of determination and eagerness, such as they had
not on any previous occasion exhibited.   A very warm and
bloody encounter ensued, during which it is no disgrace to the
handful of British troops engaged to admit that they fell for a
moment into confusion.   They were attacked simultaneously on
both flanks, in front, and in rear ; and were forced to cut their
way through a swarm of men who, issuing from the glens, threw
themselves right in the middle of the line of baggage, and forced
back a portion of it upon the leading company of the rear-guard.
But a momentary confusion is soon rectified when officers know
their duty, and men are inured to war.

   The rear-guard was not slow in meeting with its skirmishers
their assailants on all sides, while the mass pushed at once through
that portion of the enemy which had broken the line of march ; and
then the retreat was conducted with as much celerity as a regard
to the safety of the wounded would permit.   In this affair the
loss on the side of the English was very severe.   Next day's re-
turns showed that, between the flank patrols and the rear-guard,
twenty-nine men had been killed and ninety-one wounded ; and
among the former was numbered an officer of great merit and

still higher promise, Captain Wyndham, of the 35th Native Infantry. Seeing a wounded soldier unable to get on, he dismounted and lent him his horse. But Captain Wyndham was himself lame, from a previous hurt; and could not, therefore, when the rush of the enemy was the fiercest, keep up with his own people in their retreat: and the consequence was, that he, who had generously relinquished an advantage in order that a poor wounded comrade should not be lost, was himself overtaken by the savages that hung upon the rear of his party, and after a brave resistance, slain.

The division halted for the night at a point in the pass which seemed to offer rather more facilities of defence than the rest. This measure was the more necessary, that doolies and other means of transport for the sick and wounded had begun to grow scarce; and, happily for all concerned, no attempt was made to annoy the encampment. Neither was the march of the morrow interrupted, though performed for ten miles through a country little less dangerous than that which had just been traversed. A good deal of baggage had been lost the day before. If the animals be shot, or their drivers forsake them, it is impossible for the rear-guard of an army, pressed upon by a resolute enemy, to prevent this; indeed, considering the difficulties of ground to which our men were exposed on the present occasion, the only real subject of wonder is, that the whole of the baggage was not sacrificed. Be this, however, as it may, the column enjoyed, on the 30th of October, an entire exemption from molestation. A few shots, and those entirely harmless, were exchanged between the flank patrols and some straggling Afghans, whose paucity was accounted for by the assumption that the Ooloos were too busy dividing the spoil in the rear, to think of the less safe, though hardly less characteristic employment, of harassing the Feringhees in the front.

The highest point in the succession of passes that intervene between Bootkak and Jellalabad had by this time been surmounted. The march of the 3rd was therefore upon a declivity all the way; and it terminated about two in the afternoon, by introducing the column into a romantic, and, comparatively speaking, fertile strath of considerable extent, and studded with towers and hamlets. This was the valley of Gundamuck, one

of Shah Shujah's military posts; where, in a cantonment built for
their accommodation, he kept two of his own regiments, one of
cavalry, the other of infantry, with a corps of Jezailchees, or
riflemen—all under European officers. It was overspread with
vegetation, and feathered here and there with wood; among which
were fruit-trees of different kinds in abundance, and vines, of
which the produce was delicious; and a clear but shallow stream
ran with a broken current through the midst of it. It is scarcely
necessary to add, that such a scene was beheld by the hardy men
who gazed upon it with positive delight. For eighteen successive days they had toiled through the heart of bleak and
arid mountains. Beneath their feet lay a loose shingle, inter-
mixed with large stones, such as torrents roll onwards in their
course, and leave high and dry when the strength of the water
recedes; while above them and around, uprose walls of granite,
surmounted by jagged peaks, or broken cliffs, on which not so
much as a blade of grass grew. The contrast was therefore exceedingly striking; and the travellers relished it the more, that
there seemed some prospect of obtaining here the rest of which
they stood in need, while the addition of fruit and vegetables to
their diet promised as much to benefit the health of the men, as
it conduced in every possible way to gratify their tastes.

The cantonment, or barrack, which had been erected for the
Shah's troops occupied the summit of an extensive table-land,
which occurred about the centre of the valley. Close to these
huts the tents of Sale's brigades were pitched, and though the
inmates felt themselves comparatively secure, the same precautions were adopted to guard against surprise as if an enemy had
been beside them. Piquets outline and inline were on duty
day and night, and care was taken not only to prevent straggling
at a distance, but to hinder suspicious-looking strangers from
penetrating in any numbers within the line of sentries. Strict
orders were issued, likewise, to officers commanding corps, that
they would caution their men against plundering, and punish
every act of the sort on the instant; in a word, everything was
done which prudence and humanity could suggest to preserve
discipline among the troops, and to conciliate by fair dealing in
business, and kind treatment otherwise, the good will of the inhabitants.

These laudable endeavours did not fail to produce the desired result. Chief after chief inhabiting the different castles round sent in to signify their submission, and the camp was supplied with provisions of every sort, for which the parties bringing it were paid on a liberal scale. One man alone, Meer Afzal Khan by name, held aloof: and against his tower, which stood upon an eminence about four miles distant from the cantonment, Sir Robert Sale determined to send an expedition. The movement took place on the 9th of November, and was thus far successful that the fort was evacuated by its garrison as soon as the brigade approached; but the chief with his retainers escaped to the mountains, about fifteen only being cut to pieces by the cavalry. That night the troops slept in and around the castle; and on the morrow, leaving two hundred Khyberrees, under Lieutenant Gerrard, to keep possession, the remainder returned to camp.

CHAPTER XIV.

Bad tidings from Cabul—March—Arrival in Camp of unlooked-for Visitors—
Sharp Action—Approach Jellalabad.

THE division had now been nearly three weeks without any
tidings from Cabul. No convoys nor solitary messengers followed them, nor had any orders been received of a later date
than the 16th of October; and the minds of men were beginning
to be uncomfortable, an apprehension gaining ground that the
communication between their comrades in the Afghan capital
and the provinces could not, without some change of system, be
kept open. Fears, too, were experienced and expressed lest the
discontent which they all saw to prevail ere they set out upon
their homeward progress should have come to a head, and a
general rising taken place. But it was not till the morning of
the 7th that anything occurred tending in the most remote degree to give consistency to these suspicions. Moreover, when
men set themselves to inquire into the source of the various rumours that spread through the camp, the result was in every instance unsatisfactory. Everybody had heard something, yet
nobody could name his informer; such an informer at least as
might be supposed to have access to sources of intelligence that
were not open to the rest. On the 7th, however, a chief, supposed to be in Shah Shujah's interests, and who had undertaken
to guard the Jugdulluck pass till Sir William Macnaghten, the
envoy, should have passed through, sent to inform Sir Robert
Sale that there had been a revolt at Cabul, and much hard fighting, but that the Shah's troops and the Feringhees were victorious. Now there was just enough in this communication to
increase the anxiety of the brigade, certainly not to allay it.
No particulars of the fight or of the victory were stated; and
whether from the manner of the messenger, or that we are all apt
to be suspicious of such tidings of things as reach us vaguely from
afar, a distrust of the result seems involuntarily to have entered

into the minds of both officers and men.   Moreover, the tribes
in the valley began, by degrees, to put on a more insolent air;
and another messenger, who arrived on the 9th, brought letters,
as he himself stated, from Cabul, and distributed them to the
Janbazees, or Shah's regiment of cavalry.   The circumstance
was considered by no means satisfactory at head-quarter tent:
wherefore all the piquets were ordered to be strengthened at
sunset, and the officers commanding were directed to keep an eye
upon these horsemen.

So passed the interval between the morning of the 9th and the
evening of the 10th.   It was a period of considerable uneasiness
everywhere; for rumours of impending attacks began again to
pervade the camp, and the patrols of the 5th Light Cavalry,
which went round it by night, were fired upon.   Under these
circumstances, Sir Robert Sale determined to push without further delay upon Jellalabad, and to occupy the town, and keep it
till he should be correctly informed in regard to the state of
affairs at the capital.   Accordingly, instructions were given to
get the baggage animals ready, and to be prepared to strike the
tents.   But when the moment came for mustering camels and
ponies, by far the greater number were absent.   The drivers, it
appeared, had led them out, under the pretext of feeding, and
were fled, no one knew whither, and any attempt to seek for
them, even among the hills nearest at hand, was pronounced
hopeless.   This was most vexatious, yet Sale, remembering that
the safety of his troops was his first object, determined not to
abandon the plan of marching on Jellalabad.   On the contrary,
he desired that such animals as yet remained should be laden with
ammunition, hospital and commissariat stores, and that the
camp equipage and the private baggage of officers should be
committed to the keeping of the Shah's regiments which he
proposed to leave in charge of the cantonment.   Not a murmur
or word of complaint escaped any man's lips when these orders
were read: all felt that the time was come when private convenience must give way to the attainment of a public good, and all
were ready to make whatever sacrifices the urgency of circumstances might require.

In this spirit the troops addressed themselves to the packing
of their knapsacks, and the officers to the securing in the best way

they could such indispensable articles as they imagined that they
would be able to transport upon their riding horses, or about their
own persons.   The reinforcements for the piquets likewise took
up their ground, and the patrols did their duty.   Moreover, nobody was surprised to find the desultory firing about the camp
more frequent and more warm than heretofore.   Yet the bugle
never sounded, and therefore the sleepers were not called from
their lairs.   It was found, likewise, that arrangements which
could not be completed till the last moment required more time
to carry through than had been anticipated ; and the consequence
was that noon on the 11th was near at hand ere the march began.
But when begun it was conducted in the best possible order.
There might be fewer comforts in anticipation, because of the
falling off in the extent of the baggage-train ; but while the
march lasted the division learned to understand that the less of
baggage there is with an army on the move, the more pliable
and therefore the more efficient the army is.   A few shots exchanged between the rear-guard and a body of Afghans which
followed them was the only manifestation given that they were
passing through an unfriendly country ; and when the halt took
place at Futtehabad, it was found that no list, either of killed or
wounded, remained to be made up.

The column did not reach its ground till after sunset, for the
space traversed fell little short of fourteen miles ; and the arrangements for passing the night were soon made.   Songas,
with large fires burning near them, supplied the place of
tents.   But not yet had the hum of conversation ceased in the
bivouac, when two or three tent-pitchers came running in from
the rear, with tidings that the cantonments had been attacked
immediately on the departure of the brigade, and that the Shah's
Janbazees (cavalry) had joined the enemy.   A considerable sensation was produced, as may be supposed, on the receipt of this
intelligence : nor had it begun to subside when, through the dark-
ness, the sound as of a column advancing was heard ; and the
piquets stood to their arms.   By and by a body of men were
discerned, on whom the sappers—for they chanced to form the
outpost that seemed threatened—opened a heavy fire ; and it was
not suppressed without considerable difficulty, though the people
fired upon made no return.   At length, however, the firing was

stopped ; and an interchange of salutations in the English language informed the officer on duty that the intruders came as
friends, and not as enemies. A way was forthwith made for them
within the lines. They proved to be the Khyberree battalion,
who had stood by their European officers in spite of the defection
of the Janbazees ; and who, after defending the cantonments till
treason left them hopeless of doing so effectually, had marched
after the division, bringing with them only their arms, and such
ammunition as they could carry in their pouches. All the heavy
baggage thus fell into the enemy's hands, as well as two six-
pounder guns, which the Khyberrees found it impossible to
transport with them ; and everything which the plunderers did
not care to appropriate was, with the cantonments themselves,
committed to the flames.

Bad tidings were these for Sale and his men. They confirmed
the suspicion which had arisen among them, that matters could
not be going on at Cabul so favourably as the chief from Jugdulluck had represented ; and left them nothing to look for,
throughout the remainder of their progress, except hard knocks.
No man's heart failed him, however, nor was any thought entertained, except of winning and holding Jellalabad as long as it
might be judged advisable to do so. Wherefore, sharing their
fires with the new comers, the troops lay down again, and slept,
well guarded by their outposts, till about six o'clock on the
following morning, when the word was passed to rouse and take
their places.

The dawn had not broken when the troops stood to their arms,
and it was still grey twilight when the line of march was formed ;
but, for obvious reasons, there was no purpose of quitting the
ground till there should be light enough to discern objects at a
good half-mile's distance. Men stood in the ranks, therefore,
and gazed into the sky ; till, as the morning brightened, other
objects, to the full as exciting, arrested their attention. They
looked to the hills, by which a good way off the site of the
encampment was girdled in, and saw that those behind, as well
as on the right and left, were covered with Afghans. There had
been no such gathering of mountaineers at any other stage in
their progress ; and the spirit which actuated them was soon
made manifest by the dropping of long shots into the very bivouac.

ι

"We shall have warm work presently," said one to another, particularly among the companies which formed the rear-guard; and warm work sure enough they had: for scarcely had the column moved off—the baggage under its escort making ready to follow—when down from the heights on the right and left rushed the enemy, while a cloud of people coming up from behind soon formed the arc of the bow; and the whole opened upon the handful of brave men that faced them a very storm of fire.

It was beautiful to witness the coolness and perfect order with which the rear-guard, commanded that day by Lieut.-Colonel Dennie, offered a front to the assailants in every direction. The road running amid frequent declivities offered good cover for the parties which held it; while the piquets on either flank extended and maintained a sharp skirmish among the rocks. They were fed, too, with great judgment, as often as they seemed in danger of being overpowered; and Captain Oldfield, with his squadron, never lost an opportunity of dashing at such of the Afghans as ventured to descend into the low ground, and pushing them back again to the mountains. Thus, fighting in a sort of semicircle, in loose order, but with full reliance on one another, some three hundred men kept as many thousands at bay; never giving ground except for a moment, and then only to recover it again, till the well-known bugle-call, begun near the bivouac, and taken up from point to point round the valley, warned them to move on.

The object of this standing skirmish was to cover the march of the baggage animals, which moved in safety behind the flanking piquets, and gradually passed out of danger. Then, and not till then, the rear-guard took ground in the same direction, preserving its order intact, however, and taking advantage of every rock, stone, and undulation of the ground to give its fire effectively, and thus to keep the pursuers at a distance. And so the affair proceeded for about four miles. But here a village presented itself, upon which the hills closed in on either side; and to get them through the gorge as speedily as possible became with Colonel Dennie an object of paramount importance. Moreover, having reconnoitred the country beyond, and seeing that it was open and convenient for cavalry, he determined to conduct the operation in such a manner as might inspire the Afghans with an overweening confidence, and thus lure them to their destruction. He therefore directed the cavalry to pass through at a hand-gallop, and to form up in line under cover of a shoulder of one of the hills, so that they might be in a condition to act with effect should events befal as he anticipated. The bugles then sounded for the infantry, first to halt, then to advance firing, and lastly, when the enemy as usual were fleeing before them, to face about, and run with all speed through the village and the enclosures round it. Everything was done with the accuracy of a parade manœuvre ; and the results, as regarded the Afghans, fulfilled Dennie's expectations. They did not at first seem to understand what the Feringhees were about. They halted, indeed, soon after the onward rush of the rear-guard had ceased ; but were manifestly at a loss what to do when they saw the very men, who but a moment before had chased them with the eagerness of conquerors, running as if for life, when there was no man in pursuit of them. By degrees they recovered their self-possession ; and then, as if impressed with the conviction that they had achieved a great victory, they set up one of their fiendish howls, and followed helter-skelter. It was precisely the movement for which Colonel Dennie had made his arrangements. On rushed the Afghans in a dense throng, leaving village, and broken ground, and finally the gorge of the pass behind them, and away over the open valley, their whole souls, as it appeared, being intent on the destruction of the escort and the plunder of the baggage. But scarcely were they clear of the spurs of the two hills, which form, as it were, the horns of the crescent, ere Captain Oldfield's cavalry, bringing their right shoulders up, gave the spur to their chargers and were among them. At the same time a rasselah of Anderson's irregular horse, which Sir Robert Sale, observing the nature of the country as he passed, had sent back, fell upon them from the opposite side ; and the slaughter was tremendous. Not once, since the commencement of the march from Bootkak, had the Afghans received such a lesson. The sappers, whom Dennie had formed to support the cavalry, joined also in the charge ; and, following the fugitives, who took to the mountains, slew them in great numbers. It was said of the British horsemen that day, that their right arms were

wearied with the blows which they struck; and the quantity of
dead that might be seen scattered over the face of the valley
proved that they had not struck at random.

From that time, till it arrived within three miles of Jellalabad,
the rear-guard sustained no annoyance whatever. The enemy
seemed to have become satisfied all at once that, though retiring,
Sir Robert Sale's little army was not defeated; and they therefore contented themselves with following at so respectful a distance that no exchange of shots could take place. Indeed, ten
miles of way in an open country, and over a continuous descent,
offered few facilities for the sort of warfare in which they were
the most skilful; and when the road, at the termination of these,
became again difficult and contracted, they appeared very little
disposed to take advantage of it. Once, and only once, led on
by some of the Janbazees who had deserted at Gundamuck, they
advanced within very long range and began to fire. But their
shot did not tell; and Colonel Dennie, in consequence, without
pausing to return it, marched on. He halted, indeed, and formed
up as soon as the broken ground was cleared, offering them
battle, should they be disposed to accept it. But no such humour
was present with them. Wherefore the rear-guard, following in
the footsteps of their comrades who had gone before, moved on,
till, without the occurrence of any other adventure, they arrived
at Jellalabad.

CHAPTER XV.

Jellalabad—Conflagrations at Night—Sortie in the Morning.

JELLALABAD, the winter-residence of the kings of Cabul since
the Doorannee empire became consolidated, is situated in a valley
of considerable extent, and of great comparative beauty and
fertility. It is the capital of a province which stretches west
and east from the Kotah of Jugdulluck to the mouth of the
Khyber pass; and north and south from the hills which intervene between it and Kafristan, to the Safed Koh, which shuts it
out from Khuram. The valley itself may measure about eight-
and-twenty miles in length, with an average breadth of three
or four miles; and is, especially towards the Khyber extremity,
in a high state of cultivation. Besides numerous lesser streams,
three considerable rivers adorn and fertilise it; namely, the
Cabul river, which flows near the town; the Surkh Rud, or Red
River, which joins the main river at a place called Darmita; and
the Kara-Su, or Black River, which a little east of Bala Bagh
unites with the Surkh Rud. Between Bala Bagh (a town of some
importance) and Jellalabad numerous castles and villages intervene.
The face of the valley, moreover, in that direction, is well wooded
with forest-trees; and the scenery, closed in on all sides by
magnificent mountain-ranges, is attractive in the extreme. But
immediately around Jellalabad itself an arid desert spreads.
This, to persons accustomed to European arrangements, may
seem a strange peculiarity in the disposition of a town which,
because of the comparative salubrity of its climate, had been
chosen as the winter-residence of the court; yet in the East it is
not uncommon: for all that the prince seeks in such places is
exemption from the intense cold of a higher latitude; and a
sandy plain is more likely to afford this than a rich valley,
intersected by water-courses, and therefore inviting frost, so to
speak, or filling the air with damp exhalations.

The town, originally a place next in importance only to

Candahar and Cabul, had, through the ravages of war and the operation of other causes, fallen in 1841 into complete decay. It seemed, indeed, as if at intervals there had been some political necessity for curtailing its *enceinte*, for not fewer than three distinct circles of ramparts, all broken down, might be traced ; and the town itself, little better than a ruin, stood within the innermost of them. Like other Afghan cities of note, Jellalabad had its Balla Hissar : half palace, half citadel. But the Balla Hissar in the present instance, instead of standing apart from the town, as at Cabul, stood in the heart of it ; forming with its bare walls a sort of innermost town of all, and furnishing but indifferent accommodation to such as might be in the habit of dwelling there.

Uninviting to the gaze of the ordinary traveller as this dilapidated city might have appeared, to the eyes of the brave but sorely harassed handful of troops who, on the 12th of November, 1841, approached it weary and foot-sore, it offered many and great attractions. They had been accustomed to think of it amid watchings and battles as a place of at least temporary rest ; and now, in spite of the unfavourable turn which things seemed to have taken around them, they still hoped to find there repose from their toil. Not so was it with the natives. They seem never to have calculated on so bold a measure as the occupation of Jellalabad by Sale's brigade. They believed that the Feringhees were on their march to their own polluted country ; and hence every village, which the force approached and passed, sent out its armed men, more or less numerous, to assist in harassing the unbelievers. Wherefore, when, instead of encamping in the open fields, with a view of renewing his march on the morrow, Sir Robert Sale turned the head of his column towards the nearest city gate, the astonishment both of the dwellers in the town, and of the inhabitants of the villages near it, seemed to deprive them of all self-possession. As many of the citizens as could escape, fled through the opposite gates, without making so much as a show of resistance ; and thus the place was won, and whatever stores both of provisions and ammunition might happen to be deposited there, fell into the hands of the brigade, without so much as a musket-shot having been fired.

It was high time that the troops should reach this or some

other place of temporary relaxation. The stock of provisions in
hand being taken account of, was found to suffice for no more
than two days' consumption, and how to obtain a supply seemed,
when the subject came to be maturely considered, a matter
by no means easy of adjustment. There was neither difficulty
nor any hesitation in putting all ranks upon half rations ; and
all ranks, whether soldiers or civilians, prepared to contract their
appetites without a murmur. But pinch as they might, two
days' provisions held out but a slender prospect of existence to
people begirt, as was this gallant little force, by barbarous
enemies. For scarcely were they within the walls, when swarms
of Afghans appeared on every side, surrounding the town, and
uttering yells and cries, discordant and loud enough to awaken
the dead. Moreover, under cover of the many broken parapets
and buildings of various sorts, which abutted upon the place,
stragglers approached within ear-shot of the sentries, and vented
their fury in all manner of threats, which they professed themselves determined to execute, unless the town were abandoned.
And as the city wall was full of breaches, and had no ditch
before it such as deserved the name, serious apprehensions were
entertained lest, after dark, they might endeavour to force their
way into the town by mere weight of numbers. To provide
against this every necessary precaution was taken. Guards were
planted at each of the gates, which gave sentries enough to communicate at short intervals round the whole of the circuit ;
while in a sort of square or place in the centre of the town,
whence streets passed off to the several outlets, a strong piquet
was planted, with orders to send support to every point where
there should be heavy firing or other evidence of hostile operations. The rest of the little army was kept well in hand, the
men lying down by companies, having their officers near them ;
and all slept accoutred, with their weapons near, so that they
might be ready to turn out and defend themselves at a moment's
warning.

While the troops, after eating a scanty meal, found in sleep
the refreshment of which they stood sorely in need, the commandants of corps, with Sir Robert Sale at their head, met to
consider as to the steps which it would be judicious to take
amid the remarkable circumstances by which they were sur-

rounded. There were no differences of opinion in regard to the
necessity which had arisen of holding their ground where they
were, till orders from head-quarters should reach them; but a
question presented itself as to whether it would be better to keep
possession of the whole of the town, or retire within the citadel,
and there maintain themselves. They who argued for this latter
course pointed out that the town, were it even in a defensible
state, was too extensive for their force ; and that so far was it from
being defensible, that the whole of the bastions were in ruins,
the curtains themselves being pierced by various breaches. Now
the citadel, or Balla Hissar, though most imperfectly fortified,
was at all events encircled by a wall ; and, offering more than
sufficient accommodation for the troops, might be held with a
considerable saving of watchfulness and consequent exhaustion,
by a garrison well concentrated, and therefore effective in all
emergencies. It is said, I know not how truly, that at first the
leanings of the council of war were decidedly in that direction.
But a wiser policy prevailed in the end. Voices explained, that
by giving up the town you made a virtual acknowledgment of
weakness, which in the presence of a barbarous enemy is especially to be deprecated ; and that any advantage which might be
gained by a concentration of your strength would be more than
counterbalanced by the cover which the assailants would find
among the houses, and through the lanes and streets that were
abandoned to them. It is but justice to the memory of the brave
and somewhat ill-used Dennie to explain that of the latter opinion
he was the chief advocate; and well was it for the " illustrious
garrison" that, after a good deal of discussion, it prevailed.

Having settled this point, the next course resolved upon was,
that no time ought to be lost in putting the defences of the town
in the most perfect state of which they might appear capable.
To set about an operation so delicate, however, in the face of the
armed hordes which swarmed in the neighbourhood, was felt to
be impracticable ; and a determination was therefore come to of
hazarding a sally on the following day, and driving them to a
distance. And this was the more necessary, that from the summits of certain rising grounds, particularly from a rocky hill on
the southern face of the town, they managed to annoy the garrison, and to put the lives of the sentries in jeopardy, by a con-

tinual fire of matchlocks.   Accordingly, the brigade orderly-
book of that night contained instructions that a sally should take
place on the following morning through the southern gate; that
Lieut.-Colonel Monteith, C.B., 35th Native Infantry, should
command ; that he should have under his orders three hundred
men of the 13th, three hundred of the 35th, one hundred sappers,
the whole of the cavalry, two guns of Abbott's battery, and a
body of Jezalchees ; and that after sweeping the enemy from the
heights, whence they contrived to make themselves troublesome,
he should return into the city by a different gate.

In no respect does the conduct of regular and disciplined
troops contrast more remarkably with that of raw levies, than
in this,—that the care which the former take to destroy nothing
which may hold out the prospect of shelter to themselves is exceeded only by their anxiety to cut down the shelter of an enemy.
Raw levies, on the other hand, seem impelled by sheer excitement to perpetrate mischief; and this night the strength of the
impulse on the Afghans was illustrated, by the wantonness with
which they set fire to every house and shed to which, as they lay
without the walls of the town, they could gain access.   The
British troops, from their billets and quarters in the city, looked
abroad upon a sheet of flame, which was fed by habitations which
the enemy, had they been prudent, would have sought to protect,
and the besieged made it their business, on the first convenient
opportunity, to destroy.   Yet the incendiaries, so far from seeming to regret the outrage which they had committed, manifestly
rejoiced in it.   The sentries on the walls saw groups of them
dancing round each conflagration like demons.   They heard also
the wild shouts amid which the savages continued throughout the
whole night to multiply their execrations and threats of torture
to the unbelievers ; and which they ceased to pour forth only
after the flames had consumed all the material that they found to
feed upon.   And then there was a profound silence : for the
Afghan, though he frequently indulges in night attacks, or, as
he calls them, chapoas, seems to have no relish for fighting
through the hour before dawn, which, among the soldiers of
European armies, is generally considered the most suitable for
the commencement of a fray.   On the contrary, it is then that,
wearied with his nocturnal operations, he seems on all occasions

to sleep the most soundly, and is, in consequence, the most exposed to the sort of rousing which Sir Robert Sale had determined to administer to him.

Where a field of operations is strange to one of two parties,
and the other may be assumed to be familiarly acquainted with
all its features, the former, if undertaking an offensive operation,
will take care to set about it in broad day. Acting upon this
principle, Sir Robert Sale kept his columns of sortie in hand till
the sun was fully risen; and thus enabled Colonel Monteith, to
whom the privilege of leading had been entrusted, to survey
accurately and carefully the ground on which he was about to
act. He looked down from the flat roof of one of the loftiest of
the houses upon a plain, varied here and there with gardens and
other enclosures, some of which came near to the Cabul gate,
and were dotted with castles, of which they seem to form the
pleasure-grounds. He saw likewise, where, in another direction,
at the distance of perhaps a quarter of a mile from the wall,
the river poured its waters, and, turning round, examined the
hills towards the south, which commanded the town completely,
though at a considerable range. The hills, as well as the gardens
and the flat country beyond, were crowded with Afghans. There
could not be fewer than five thousand warriors at the least; and,
in spite of the entire absence of discipline, according to the
European sense of that term, which characterized them, they
presented a formidable appearance, being stout men and well
armed. All the various features in the scene, as well as the dispositions which the enemy had made for the purpose of turning
them to account, Colonel Monteith took time to examine; and
then he proceeded in a soldier-like manner to perform the duty
which was required of him.

The total amount of force put under his orders fell somewhat
short of eleven hundred men; and of these only three hundred
and fifty were Europeans. Above seven hundred, including the
ordinary guards and piquets, remained for the defence of the
place, so that the operation, however agreeable to the ordinary
course of things, could not but be regarded as a critical one.
The slightest reverse, it was felt, would tell; and if by chance
more than a reverse were to befal, the consequences must be
serious. Wherefore every precaution, which circumstances ap-

peared to suggest, were adopted to prevent disaster. The troops within the town stood to their arms. All the artillery, with the exception of the pieces which had been told off for service, were ranged along the walls, so as to cover the advance of the sortie; and opened their fire as soon as word was passed that the march was about to begin. Yet though the practice was excellent, and men and horses went down beneath it, the enemy gave no ground till the leading companies rushed out, and closed upon them with a sharp and rapid storm of musketry.

There was an enclosure outside the town, with a mansion-house and other buildings in the midst of it, to which, because Sir William Macnaghten had dwelt there during the residence, in the previous winter, of Shah Shujah's court at Jellalabad, the name of the Mission Compound had been given. There the Khyberree regiment, " faithful among the faithless found," had passed the night; and now the enemy, as if in anticipation of a movement on the side of the garrison, attacked it with great fury. The Khyberrees fought well; but were forced to give way, till the cavalry, issuing from the nearest gate, fell upon the assailants, and cut them down in great numbers. It so happened, also, that the gallant squadron of the 5th were brought into collision with the Janbazees, who had betrayed their trust at Gundamuck; and though the latter offered a stout resistance, they went down like nine-pins before the charge. Meanwhile the infantry, passing through the Cabul gate, advanced towards the hills. They were thronged with defenders, who kept up a heavy but not very effective fire; and among them was a piper, who ceased not to play upon his most unmusical instrument, regardless of the shower of balls that whistled past him. As a matter of course the piper became the subject of many a rude joke among the men of the 13th. They laughed while they took deliberate aim at him, showing, however, this much of respect to his acknowledged bravery, that in honour of him they forthwith denominated the heights " The Piper's Hill." And I do not doubt that a name, which it received during this memorable struggle, the rock still retains, even among the Afghans. It is right to add, that the piper escaped unhurt.

There was a panic among the Afghans in all quarters. The cavalry, breaking out of the enclosures, fell upon them, thronged together in the plain, and hewed them down. The infantry, after pushing the occupants of the hills from their vantage-ground, hung upon their rear, till they fled outright. They were pursued as far as the nearest of the forts, into which the victors forced their way, securing—an acceptable reward of their gallantry—the small stock of grain which it contained. And now, seeing that the purposes of the sortie had been accomplished to the utmost extent of men's wishes, the bugles sounded the recall. Slowly, and with apparent reluctance, the victorious troops obeyed the summons. By twos and threes the skirmishers closed upon the centre, and marched back to take their places with the supporting column; and the whole returned in great spirits within the city. As to the enemy, not a trace of them could be discovered as far as the eye reached. About two hundred dead bodies scattered over the plain told where they had lately been; but of living warriors not one remained to annoy, even with threats and abusive language, the gallant garrison of Jellalabad.

CHAPTER XVI.

Continuance of the Blockade.

FROM the date of this successful sally up to the 28th of November, the garrison sustained no serious molestation. An opportunity was thus afforded, of which Sir Robert Sale made excellent use, to strengthen his position, and to lay in such a stock of provisions as might enable him to hold his ground till it should be judged expedient to shift it. In order to accomplish the former of these objects, strong working-parties were employed from morning till night in filling up the breaches in the town walls, and clearing out and deepening the ditches in part of them. Every tree, likewise, which stood in the line of fire was cut down ; every wall and house and inequality in the ground levelled ; while the forts or towers which in several directions came close in upon what had been the suburbs, had their near walls beaten down, so as to render them untenable by an enemy. In like manner parapets were run up along the ramparts, sand-bags and the saddles of the baggage animals being used in their construction ; and finally, ten pieces of cannon, of various calibre, and in some instances mounted on strange carriages, with one or two mortars, were run into the bastions, and equipped for service. Meanwhile foraging parties went out under sufficient escorts, which gathered in from the villages and homesteads round about all manner of grain, sheep, fuel, and other useful articles. And the consequence was, that within the space of a few days, not only had the town become defensible against such an enemy as was likely to assail it, but the commissary, on taking account of his stock, satisfied himself that there was provision enough for a month's consumption at the rate then in use, namely, half-rations.

All this was satisfactory : nor perhaps could any one much lament, under the circumstances in which the brigade was placed, that not one drop of spirits remained in store. Undoubtedly there are cases in which ardent spirits, used as a medicine, prove

invaluable. Many a frame, exhausted and sinking, has been
sustained by the stimulus of brandy till nature had time to rally ;
but considered as an article of daily consumption, it is now universally acknowledged that ardent spirits tend only to weaken,
not to invigorate, the human constitution. But it is not easy to
persuade either soldiers or sailors of this fact ; and so long as
the English government shall continue to include a certain
portion of fire-water in the supplies which it furnishes to its
troops, the troops will demand the poison as their right—and get
it. And so long as English soldiers are encouraged and invited
to regard the habit of drinking spirits as a privilege peculiar to
their class, crime, as well as disease, will abound in the army,
whether it serve at home or abroad. In Jellalabad, however,
there were no spirits, nor could any of the places round about
supply them : and the consequence was, that throughout the continuance of this siege there was no crime, no sickness, except
from wounds,—the highest courage, the very best humour, and
a docility and quickness such as had never before been noticed,
even in the 13th Light Infantry, remarkable as that fine regiment
had long been for all the qualities which combine to form the
character of a really efficient corps.

From the 14th to the 28th of November, the garrison of
Jellalabad sustained no serious molestation by the attacks of the
enemy. Parties of Afghans hung about the place all this while, and
at night the sentries on the walls were frequently fired at ; while
from time to time a rumour spread abroad, which put both men
and officers on the alert. For example, a report would come in
over-night that the working-parties were to be attacked as soon
as they passed beyond the walls on the morrow : and a strong
covering party was directed in consequence to precede them, and
to patrol round the place, in order to guard against the hazard.
On another occasion the foragers would be threatened, perhaps
molested : whereupon the nearest guard or piquet would seize
their weapons and run to the rescue ; or the cavalry sally forth,
and with its accustomed bravery and skill, dash at twice or thrice
its own numbers, and sweep them away. But no affair of importance took place ; neither were any valuable lives wasted. One
circumstance, indeed, created a good deal of uneasiness in the
minds of those to whom it was known. On taking account of

the musket ammunition, the alarming discovery was made, that, including what the men carried in their pouches, not more than one hundred and twenty rounds per head remained. Nevertheless, no human being dreamed of desponding; indeed, the only measure which brave men so circumstanced could adopt was adopted; an order being issued that the greatest care should be taken not to throw away a shot, and therefore never to fire, except in an extremity, and then only when sure of doing so with effect.

Jellalabad was now fairly in a state of siege. The communications with both Cabul and Peshawur, though not entirely cut off, were become so insecure, that intelligence from either place reached the garrison but rarely; and, except when brought by messengers hired to conceal written billets about their persons, could not always be depended upon. On the 15th, for example, tidings arrived of a great success at Cabul, and the same evening a salute of twenty-one guns was fired in honour of the victory. But scarcely had the echoes died away among the mountains, ere news of revolts and disasters in other quarters spread abroad. It was ascertained beyond doubt, that a post at Besh-i-bolak, about twenty-five miles on the Peshawur road—which Captain Ferrirs, with a Jezalchee corps, had hitherto maintained—was forced; and Ferrirs with his men were described as retreating upon Peshawur. By and by, cossids (messengers) brought information, that the whole of the road between Bootkak and Gundamuck was blocked; that the enemy had established posts at every favourable point; and that elsewhere, from the one extremity of Afghanistan to the other, the population was in arms. Then followed tales of more battles, disastrous to the English; of the shutting-up of Shah Shujah in the Balla Hissar, and of the British army in its cantonments; of the blockade of Ghuznee, Candahar, and indeed of every post and fortress into which the English had thrown a garrison. It was impossible to say how much of importance deserved to be attached to these rumours; though some of them, particularly such as described the death or the wounds of individuals, carried with them a great air of truth. But the general effect was more and more to satisfy Sale and his followers, that, as far as their immediate safety stood affected, they must trust to the protection of Providence and their own right hands: and not a man among them seemed to desire any better guarantee for the attainment of this end, important as they all felt it to be.

For two or three days there had been a whisper in Jellalabad that the repose which the garrison enjoyed from hostile operations would soon be interrupted. More than once cautions were given to the officers on guard at the gates to be upon the alert, and the infantry slept accoutred in their quarters; the cavalry, with their horses saddled, near them. This was particularly the case during the nights of the 27th and 28th; indeed, dropping shots, which whistled by the sentries, told, that whether in large numbers or in small, an enemy was certainly near; but on the morning of the 29th all doubts were removed. There were seen advancing from the side of Cabul dense columns of men, of which the numbers were guessed not to fall short of four or five thousand, while in front of them moved a cloud of skirmishers, who, penetrating as far as the broken ground near the river side, opened a desultory fire upon the place. The garrison stood to its arms, of course: but observing that the main body showed no design of hazarding an assault; that it rather spread itself round the town, occupying a number of forts about a mile and a half distant, and taking possession of the Piper's Hill, Sir Robert Sale contented himself with abiding in a state of preparedness, and kept his troops in hand. The consequence was, that throughout that, and for two or three days succeeding it, almost all the noise and show of fighting was on the side of the Afghans. For the British troops, mindful of the caution which they had received, reserved their musketry fire with admirable coolness, and answered the enemy only with an occasional cannon shot, of which, happily for themselves, they possessed a good store.

So passed the interval between the 29th of November and the 1st of December. The enemy, encouraged by the apparent supineness of the garrison, grew from hour to hour more bold, throwing his skirmishers continually nearer to the walls, and putting an entire stop to the operations of the working parties, till at last Sir Robert Sale determined to give them a lesson; and a force, consisting of the cavalry, two nine-pounder guns, and three hundred men from each of the infantry regiments, was placed

under the command of Colonel Dennie, and desired to clear them
off. It was about one o'clock in the day when Colonel Dennie
received his instructions ; and having waited till his men had eaten
their noontide meal, he sallied forth. The cheer of the soldiers
rang through the air, and seemed to produce a great effect upon
the Afghans. Their scattered parties ran together, formed up
in a rude line, and, as soon as the head of the column appeared
through the gateway, fired a volley. It was perfectly harmless,
and can hardly be said to have been repeated, for the people who
gave it broke and fled, our troops rushing after them at the top
of their speed. The guns, also, were unlimbered, and poured
grape with murderous accuracy among the fugitives ; while the
cavalry, striking spurs into their horses, dashed among the throng,
and struck their blows, to the right and left, with excellent will.
Never was rout more complete. The enemy, scattered in all
directions, some fleeing across the plains, others making for the
river, into which repeated charges of the cavalry forced them ;
while the infantry, making no pause, carried the hills at the point
of the bayonet. About one hundred and fifty of the besiegers fell
on that day, without the loss to the troops employed against them
of a single one. And when the dawn of the morrow came in,
it was ascertained that the forts which the main body had occupied were deserted, and that the whole of the enormous masses
which came up on the 29th, with such a show of resolution, were
dissolved and gone, nobody could tell whither.

A long interval of comparative repose ensued, after this brilliant sortie, to the garrison of Jellalabad. It was occupied, as
similar periods of time had been before, in strengthening the
works, and adding to the stock of provisions ; men's minds being
kept all the while in a state of excitement—not always of a plea-
surable nature—by the rumours of battle and disaster which came
in from Cabul : for the truth began by degrees to ooze out.
The murder of Sir Alexander Burnes and his friends, and slender
guard, was already an acknowledged fact. So was the unac-
countable blunder which had permitted the commissariat fort at
Cabul, with all its valuable contents, to fall into the hands of
the enemy. And there now came in details, more or less accurate, of the ill-directed attack upon the Rekabashee fort, where
Colonel Shelton's brigade somewhat misconducted itself ; and

K

Colonel Mackerell, with other valuable officers, was slain. By and by an indistinct narrative of the disasters of the detachment stationed in the Nijrow valley began to circulate. The murder of Lieutenant Rattray, assistant political agent there, much aggravated the sufferings of his brother of the 13th Light Infantry, who still lay sick with the wound which he had received in the affair of Jugdulluck; and it tended in no respect to raise either his spirits or the spirits of his comrades, when authentic intelligence of the destruction of the whole force, with the exception of Major Pottinger and Lieutenant Houghton, both of whom had been previously wounded, reached them. Thus, from day to day, tidings disastrous and humiliating poured in upon this handful of brave men. For though they heard that a brigade had marched from Candahar for the purpose of forcing its way to Cabul, and bringing relief to the beleaguered garrison, no intelligence of its arrival reached them; and it soon came out that the relieving force had found the passes too strictly guarded, and had been obliged to retrace its steps, and seek safety within the walls of the old capital.

It is impossible for those who have not themselves had personal experience of the matter to enter into or understand the feelings of men situated as were at this time Sir Robert Sale and his followers. Isolated in a country where every human being was their enemy, or prepared to become such on the first appearance of weakness on their part; having no hope of relief from their comrades whom they had quitted, and as little that an armed force from the provinces would come to succour them; without supplies of any sort, except such as they could procure for themselves; and above all, knowing that one protracted and desperate battle would leave them, whether victorious or beaten, without a round of musket-ammunition wherewith to defend their lives, they would have been either more or less than men had not anxiety weighed upon their spirits. Moreover, it is marvellous with what effect rumours, whether sinister or the reverse, tell when circulated among people in their plight. Eager to believe the best, yet with natural waywardness distrustful both of their informants and of their own wishes, they receive the many and contradictory tales which reach them with a strange mixture of feeling. But when upon the 17th a messenger came in, and Sir Robert Sale, having read the despatch, put it into his pocket and made no mention of its contents, men's surmises became more dark, because more vague, than ever; and though each, when questioned, could give no good authority for what he said, there was scarcely an individual in the place whose mouth was not filled with tales of disaster. At last the rumour began to circulate that the British army in Cabul had capitulated, and that Sir William Macnaghten had agreed to evacuate Afghanistan on condition that their march to the provinces should be unmolested. No words can describe the sensation which this rumour, in whatever source originating, created. Shame, sorrow, indignation, were the feelings uppermost in every man's heart; and the speech of all was strongly tinctured with the tone which such feelings give. The result was, that the garrison of Jellalabad came, as if by common consent, to the conclusion that there could be no truth whatever in the story. "They may have mismanaged their business,—that is very probable; they may have sustained great loss, and have before them the prospect of much suffering and many privations; but to tell us that they have capitulated—the thing is out of the question." So argued these gallant fellows, judging of others from themselves; and then dismissing all uneasy thoughts, as far as it was possible so to do, from their minds, they returned to their daily tasks of working, and foraging, and laying in stores of every kind, with all the zeal and good humour which had characterised their proceedings from the outset.

CHAPTER XVII.

Bad News—Arrival of Dr. Brydon—His Narrative.

So passed the latter months of 1841. They had been pregnant
with events of very deep moment to every individual in the
brigade : yet the progress of time soon showed that other and
still more startling incidents were to be born of them. January,
1842, came in with frightful tidings in his hand. The officers
of the garrison had celebrated Christmas Day, first by reverently
attending divine worship, and then by dining together after the
custom of their country, and remembering in their talk the
friends and relatives whom they might never perhaps see again.
Their beverage was water; yet they drank it to the healths of
many far away, and were as happy, with a sobered joy, as they
could expect to be apart from the society of those dearest to
them. And here let me not forget to record to the honour of
the illustrious garrison, that regularly as the Lord's Day came
round, brigade orders called both officers and men together, that
in his own name and in the names of his comrades, one of themselves might present to their Father which is in heaven their
common sacrifice of prayer and praise. It was a righteous custom,
and produced upon all concerned the happiest effect. It sobered
while it encouraged all, from the highest to the lowest, teaching
them to feel that the lives of the brave are in the hands of Him
who gave them; and that the best preparation which men can
make for battle and for death comes out of a humble yet hopeful
reliance on the mercy, as well as on the power, of the Most
High. Nor do I think that I go beyond the line of sober truth
if to the prevalence of this right feeling among them, aided by
the happy absence of that bane of a soldier's usefulness, spirituous
liquors, and the encouraged use of them, I attribute the patience,
the good-humour, the unwearied zeal, which from the beginning
to the end of the siege characterised the behaviour of all classes,
and rendered the garrison of Jellalabad, though few in number,

invincible.   Had the same tempers prevailed at Cabul, and the
same wisdom been exhibited in the encouragement of them, who
can doubt that the fate of General Elphinstone's corps would
have been different?

New Year's Day, 1842, is marked in a journal which lies
before me with two emphatic words, "All quiet." Their meaning is, that no shots were fired, that no enemy showed himself,
that no untoward rumours occurred to disturb the equanimity of
the garrison, and that within the walls and without things held
their accustomed course.   Quiet, in a besieged city, is a state of
things which has no existence ; for the spade and the pickaxe are
at work continually ; and guards are watchful, and sentinels
much on the alert, whether there be any visible object of suspicion near them or the reverse.   On the 1st of January, precisely as on other days, the routine of life went on ; and from
hour to hour the defences of the place became more formidable.
But the 2nd brought with it ample ground of uneasiness and
alarm.   A letter from Major Pottinger announced that Sir William Macnaghten was murdered ; and described, hurriedly, the
terrible results that ensued from that act of treason.   And while
men yet held their breath through horror of such tidings, another
messenger brought word that the Candahar brigade had been
stopped by the snow, and fallen back again after having penetrated as far as Ghuznee.   Finally, a despatch from Akbar Khan
to one of the chiefs in the neighbourhood was intercepted and
brought in ; from which Captain M'Gregor learned that a holy
war was proclaimed ; and that all believers were adjured, in the
name of the Prophet, to rise against the infidels, "whose chief,"
continued this memorable despatch, "I have slain with mine own
hand, as you, I trust, will in like manner slay the chief of the
Feringhees in Jellalabad."

There was horror and extreme indignation among those who
listened to these recitals ; but not one pulse beat the more hurriedly.   They felt, indeed, more and more, that their lives were
in their own keeping ; for they who had murdered the envoy
while sitting with them in friendly conference, breaking through
their national respect for the rites of hospitality, and violating
the sanctity that in all lands attaches to the person and character
of an ambassador, were not likely to spare the lives of soldiers

who had resisted them so long and so daringly. The little conclave therefore broke up, the determination of its members being additionally strengthened ; and forth, as usual, went foragers on the prowl, and grass-cutters to provide food for the horses and camels. No great while elapsed, moreover, ere signs of a coming storm began to show themselves. Parties of armed men were seen, now at a distance, now hovering about the place ; and on the 7th one of these fell upon the cavalry grass-cutters, and ere assistance could be sent slew three of them. Immediately horsemen of the 5th cavalry rode to the rescue ; but they arrived too late, and brought back with them two out of the three headless trunks of their unlucky attendants. The poor fellows were buried within the ditch ; and care was taken not to trust any more of their number abroad, except a sufficient escort attended them.

The 8th of January passed somewhat in gloom. Hopes had been entertained that ere this something would have been heard of the force from Peshawur ; which was understood to have been warned for a march up the country, but of the coming of which no signs appeared. The 9th was rendered memorable by the unexpected arrival before the town of a small band of horsemen, bearers of a flag of truce, and messengers, as to the officer on guard they described themselves to be, from Cabul. They were conducted into the presence of Sir Robert Sale, and produced a letter, written in English, and subscribed with General Elphinstone's name. It contained the announcement that between the writer and Akbar Khan a convention had been established, whereby General Elphinstone had agreed to evacuate the country, and that the evacuation was to begin from Jellalabad. The garrison was accordingly directed to march immediately, with its arms, stores, and ammunition, for Peshawur ; because the force in Cabul had agreed not to commence its movement towards the provinces, till it should have been assured that General Sale and his people were beyond the frontier. "Everything," continued this remarkable despatch, "has been done in good faith. You will not be molested on your way ; and to the safe-conduct which Akbar Khan has given, I trust for the passage of the troops under my immediate orders through the passes."

There was no mistake here. The document was a genuine document, and the signature that of one with whose handwriting all were familiar; and the orders were as peremptory as ever came from the head-quarters of an army or a corps. What was to be done? Were such orders, so issued, to be obeyed? A man less resolute than he whose fall on the banks of the Sutlej is yet mourned as a national calamity, would have obeyed such orders at once. There might be risk in the march, but risks soldiers are trained to encounter; and perhaps, if the scales were fairly held, the hazards attending a retreat out of the country might appear less serious than must attend the endeavour to hold on. But Sale had other thoughts in his mind than his own personal peril, or even peril to the lives of his followers. He thought of the honour of his country, and of the wisdom, in a political point of view, of not abandoning altogether the fruits of the triumphs of 1839; and, full of these convictions, he called together the commandants of his several corps, and the heads of the several departments which served under him. A sort of council of war was held, in which the same noble spirit that animated Sale was found to prevail. They examined the despatch narrowly; saw that it was dated not fewer than eleven days back; and came to the resolution " that it would not be prudent to act upon such a document; and that the garrison would therefore abide where it was till further orders."

It would have been idle to think of concealing from the troops the contents of the communication which had reached the general. Nobody, indeed, seems to have thought it necessary to make the attempt; for the men were as resolute as the officers; and both classes held up their hands in amazement when the capitulation of five thousand disciplined soldiers to any conceivable number of barbarians was announced to them as an affair accomplished. Moreover, the men were ready either to march or abide where they were, according as those to whom they looked for guidance should judge expedient; and when the latter and wiser determination was announced to them, they received it with a cheer, and turned to their work with renewed alacrity. Probably the annals of war offer few parallels to the state of discipline and mutual confidence in each other to which this handful of brave men—Asiatics equally with Europeans—had been brought. The men believed that their officers would always decide wisely for them. The officers believed that the men would accomplish whatever they were desired to attempt; and the consequence was that, amid dangers and difficulties of the most trying kind, the spirits of both classes kept up.

For some days previously there had been considerable uneasiness, because of the lack of information from Peshawur. Hitherto, though neither troops nor stores came from that quarter, communications in writing had been pretty regularly sent in; and more than once the commandant or political agent had managed to convey to General Sale a supply of money. The money was well used in bribing certain chiefs and heads of villages in the districts round to send grain, and sheep, and cattle, for the use of the garrison. But latterly no despatches of any kind had arrived; and as the funds at Sale's disposal were exhausted, apprehensions began to be entertained lest supplies should run short. It was therefore a pleasant break in the monotony of their existence when, towards evening on the 11th, forty horsemen, part of the train of Turabas Khan, a friendly chief, sought admittance into the town. They had come from Peshawur by the Lalpoora road, and were the bearers, not only of letters, but of treasure to the amount of twenty-one thousand rupees.

It was something to have received a supply of money. In Afghanistan, as in most other parts of the world, where money happens to be scarce, little service is to be procured; where it is abundant, every man, woman, or child whom you meet is more or less amenable to your bidding. The acquisition of this increase to his slender store gave therefore to Sir Robert Sale an assurance that not yet would he run the risk of being starved into a surrender. But he would have given the whole of the rupees, perhaps the amount twice told, for a moderate supply of musket ammunition; of which the stock, in spite of great care in husbanding and reserving it, was beginning to diminish fast. Moreover, just about this period, as if to fill up the amount of his difficulties, suspicions began for the first time to be entertained regarding the fidelity of the Jezalchees. It did not exactly appear upon what ground these suspicions rested. Nobody could say that he had either seen or heard ought in the behaviour of the men which would justify him in bringing so grave a charge against them, as that they had meditated proceedings hostile to the garrison or were in communication with the enemy. Nevertheless, when a suspicion of the kind contrives by any means to spring up, it is a very difficult matter to get rid of it; and of all the feelings which can affect men circumstanced as at that time were Sale and his brigade, it is hard to conceive any more distressing than the doubt of the trustworthiness of those with whom they are associated.

Working parties busied themselves all day long during the 11th and the 12th in digging a ditch round the bastion on the north-west angle of the town, that being the point on which the acting engineer saw that the place was weakest. They were thus engaged, their arms being piled near them, and the cavalry, with horses saddled, ready to gallop forth to their support, when a little after noon on the 13th, one of the sentries on that part of the wall which faced Gundamuck and the road from Cabul, called aloud that he saw a mounted man in the distance. In a moment glasses were levelled in this direction, and there, sure enough, could be distinguished, leaning rather than sitting upon a miserable pony, a European, faint, as it seemed, from travel, if not sick, or perhaps wounded. It is impossible to describe the sort of thrill which ran through men's veins as they watched the movements of the stranger. Slowly he approached; and strange as it may appear, it is nevertheless true, that Colonel Dennie foretold the nature of the tidings of which he was the bearer: for it is a fact, which every surviving officer of the 13th will vouch for, that almost from the first Colonel Dennie had boded ill of the force left in Cabul; and that subsequently to the receipt of the earliest intelligence which told of the warfare in which they were engaged, and of the disastrous results to which it led, he repeatedly declared his conviction, that to a man the army would be destroyed. His words were, " You 'll see. Not a soul will escape from Cabul except one man; and he will come to tell us that the rest are destroyed." Under such circumstances it is very little to be wondered at, if men's blood curdled while they watched the advance of the solitary horseman; and the voice of Dennie sounded like the response of an oracle, when he exclaimed, " Did I not say so ? here comes the messenger."

Colonel Dennie spoke the truth. An escort of cavalry being sent out to meet the traveller, he was brought in bleeding and

faint, and covered with wounds; grasping in his right hand the
hilt, and a small fragment of a sword which had broken in the
terrible conflict from which he was come. He proved to be Dr.
Brydon, whose escape from the scene of slaughter had been marvellous, and who at the moment believed himself to be, and was
regarded by others, as the sole survivor of General Elphinstone's once magnificent little army.

The tale of the disastrous retreat from Cabul, and of the
frightful massacre of the ill-commanded troops which set forth
upon it, has been told too often, and with too much breadth of
detail, to permit a repetition of the narrative here. Enough is
done when I state, that from the lips of their wounded comrade,
as soon as care and wholesome diet had in some degree recovered
his strength, the officers of the Jellalabad garrison received
an account of all that had befallen, from the fatal blunders which
characterised the first endeavours that were made to put down
the revolt, up to the signing of the treaty of armistice, and its
immediate violation by the Afghan chiefs. Dr. Brydon told
how the column set forth, disorganised and cowed at the very
beginning of its march; how first the baggage, and by and by
the soldiers, were set upon by the enemy that tracked their
steps; how they fought their way through the Koord Cabul,
some dropping under the fire that was showered upon them from
the rocks, others perishing of cold amid the snow which constituted their beds at night. He described the wavering and
imbecility of the leaders; the insubordinate conduct of the men;
their desperate valour on all occasions, which led, however, to
no results, because there was no mind present to direct it wisely;
and last of all, the treachery of Akbar Khan, who, enticing the
General, with almost all the other officers of rank, into his
power, left the wreck of the army without any one to guide it.
When matters arrived at this pass there was an end to discipline, to order, and of course to strength. The troops straggled
forward by parties as far as Jugdulluck. There, at the end of
the narrow ascent, an abattis of prickly pear had been thrown
across the road, in their effort to force a way through which
multitudes perished. At last, all the sepoys and camp-followers
having died, some of cold and fatigue, others by bullets or the
sword, a miserable remnant of the 44th regiment, with about

forty European officers, arrived in the vicinity of Gundamuck, having marched all night, and fought a battle for the passage of the river. Here it would seem that some of the officers and the men parted company. About twelve, who were better mounted than the rest, rode on with a few cavalry which had survived the march. One by one they dropped off, till six only remained, and these pulled up to rest for a short space at Futtehabad. It was a fatal measure, into which a treacherous show of kindness by the inhabitants lured them: for while they were yet eating the morsel of bread which had been ostentatiously placed before them, a band of ruffians rushed upon them and cut down two. The other four galloped off, and Dr. Brydon, who was the worst mounted of the whole, soon fell into the rear. His heart failed him, as well it might; so he quitted the road, and concealed himself for a while behind some rocks that offered shelter. But here, the thought occurred that to him there was no safety in delay; so he once more turned his jaded pony into the road, and pushed on. He soon came up with the body of one of his friends, which lay in the middle of the path terribly mutilated; and had not proceeded far beyond it ere an Afghan horseman, armed to the teeth, confronted him. There was nothing for it but to offer the best resistance which the wretched weapon by his side, and the jaded state of his starved horse, might enable him to do. He fought for his life, and in the *melée* his sword broke off by the hilt. Just then he received a wound in the knee, the pain of which caused him to stoop forward; whereupon the Afghan, supposing that he was about to draw a pistol, turned and fled. He rode on, bleeding and weak, yet thankful for the respite from death which had been granted him; and, being soon afterwards espied from the ramparts of Jellalabad, was brought in, as has just been described, to the garrison.

CHAPTER XVIII.

Continued Preparations for Defence—Construction of Corn-mills—
Earthquake.

THE horror of those to whom Dr. Brydon told his tale of blood
surpasses the power of language to describe.   They felt that the
work of slaughter must have been long ere this consummated ;
yet the cavalry were ordered to mount forthwith, and to patrol
along the Cabul road to the farthest reach which might seem to
be compatible with a regard to their own safety.   A good many
officers accompanied them ; and they had not ridden above four
miles from the town ere they came upon the mutilated remains of
the three out of Dr. Brydon's four ill-fated companions, of whom
he could give no account.   Not a straggler, however—not a living
soul, man, woman, or child—appeared either there, or as far as
the eye could reach beyond.   Wherefore the patrol, after linger-
ing about till the shadows began to deepen, turned their horses'
heads with sorrow homewards, and rejoined their comrades.
That night lanterns were suspended from poles at different points
about the ramparts : while from time to time the bugles sounded
the advance, in the hope that one or other of these beacons might
guide some wanderer to a place of rest.   But none came ; and
though on the morrow, and for several days and nights subsequently, a like course was pursued, not one man, European or
native, seemed to be alive—certainly none profited by it.

   And now, more than ever convinced that they had but themselves and the hand of Providence to look to, the " illustrious
garrison " continued to deepen their ditches, to strengthen their
ramparts, and to make every preparation which circumstances
would allow for meeting and repelling the fierce attack with
which they expected hourly to be favoured.   Occasionally a word
or look of reproach might perhaps escape them when thoughts of
what might have been done had the force from Peshawur come
up in time, entered into their minds.   They knew, what the bri-

gade stationed at Peshawur probably did not know—that every man capable of bearing arms had been summoned to the war at Cabul, and hence that the Khyber pass was left well nigh destitute of defenders.   Had the leader of the Peshawur force been but aware of that fact, he would have probably disregarded whatever cautions reached him from the provinces; and, marching upon Jellalabad, might have given a very different turn to the issues of the strife, or, at the worst, rendered the escape of General Elphinstone and his army certain.   But either his ignorance of the real state of the case, or his respect for authority (a great military principle), kept him back, and now it would have been utter madness to think of moving.   Accordingly, if a reproachful thought entered by chance into the mind of any individual attached to the garrison of Jellalabad, it referred always to days gone by, and opportunities neglected; for with reference both to the present and the future, the least reflecting of that gallant band saw that all must depend upon his own powers of endurance, and that of the comrades with whom he acted.

In coming to the conclusion that the force from Peshawur would not move at all, the garrison of Jellalabad did their comrades wrong.   There was every wish on the part of Brigadier General Wyld to go to the relief of his beleaguered fellow soldiers; and he did march as soon as the political agent would sanction the step, though only to be stopped while a vain endeavour was made to accomplish by negotiation what the sword alone had power to achieve.   The consequence was, that baffled, deceived, and overreached, two regiments of Native Infantry lingered at the foot of the pass, till such a crowd of warriors gathered for its defence, that when the attempt was made to cut a way through it failed.   So did the intermixture of civil with military authority work at every stage in the Afghan war.   So unhappy was the influence which presided over every plan for the maintenance of a commanding position in a country whereinto a British army ought never, perhaps, to have entered.

Meanwhile information in regard to the fate of the few survivors from General Elphinstone's corps began to come in.   A letter was received, on the 18th, from Captain Souter, of the 44th, which, bearing date "Tootoo, near Gundamuck," gave an ac-

count of the last struggle made by a handful of the men of his
regiment, in which they were all destroyed. Only he and Major
Griffiths, of the 37th Native infantry, survived; and they were
both prisoners in the hands of a chief, who undertook to convey
them uninjured to Jellalabad, provided he were made sure of
receiving a ransom at the rate of a thousand rupees for each.
In a moment a subscription was set on foot, and the privates of
the 13th collecting among them upwards of one thousand
rupees, the remainder were with great difficulty mustered by the
officers. A report to this effect was sent without delay to
Tootoo, whereupon the Serjeant Major of the 37th, who was
likewise a prisoner there, came over; and a second offer was
made to ransom the whole, including thirteen men of the 13th, and
fifteen, or thereabouts, of the 44th, for a lakh of rupees. With
extreme difficulty, and only by encroaching on the public funds,
the desired amount was made up. But the parties sent with it
were set upon and plundered before they reached the place of
their destination; and the next thing heard of the unhappy captives was that Akbar Khan had claimed them, and removed
them to a place of security in the Lughman valley. There were
not two opinions in the garrison respecting the robbery of the
treasure, or the cause of it. The whole was understood to be
the result of a preconcerted scheme, and the poor fellows who
had given all that they possessed to redeem their countrymen
from bondage were forced to find what consolation they might
in the consciousness of having acted for the best.

Among the chiefs whose clans dwelt in the vicinity of Jellalabad, there was one Abdool Guffoor Khan, whose aim seemed
to be to keep as far as possible on good terms with both parties.
He it was who, on receiving an exorbitant price, used to supply
the garrison with provisions; and he now so far enlarged the
circle of his friendly offices, as to become the medium of communication between General Sale's brigade and the British prisoners in the Lughman valley. These, as is well known, included the wives of all the officers who had been so imprudent
as to carry their families to Cabul; among whom were Lady
Sale and her daughter, Mrs. Sturt, now unfortunately a widow;
and to them, as well as to the officers and men, such supplies of
little luxuries were sent as their own poverty, in regard to these

matters, enabled the garrison of Jellalabad to muster. Clothing, books, and a small supply of money reached the prisoners safely, and were by them highly esteemed. But of tea there was not a grain in Jellalabad, and coffee was in like manner wanting.

Such were the principal events which left their impress as it passed on to the month of January, 1842. Stirring and important, though the reverse of exhilarating, all who survived to speak of them felt them to be; yet were they but the forerunners of others still more momentous to the handful of resolute men by whom Jellalabad was occupied. For the very first day of February gave promise, or seemed to do so, of sharper work than had yet been encountered. Numerous bodies of the enemy were observed marching from various quarters, and pushing off all in the same direction, namely, towards Lughman. The natural inference was, that there the grand muster would take place, and that when they had assembled in sufficient force to bear down, as they imagined, all resistance, Akbar Khan and his people would attack. Now though to this consummation all men looked, as to a thing sooner or later inevitable, its near approach put them a good deal upon their mettle. An order came out the same day, that all such of the camp-followers as were able to carry arms should be enrolled; and these, knowing that they would surely share the fate of their masters, cheerfully obeyed it. As many muskets and rifles as chanced to be in store (they were not very numerous, for they had accumulated chiefly out of deaths in the field) were delivered to the most enterprising, while the remainder were supplied with pikes, the heads of which were fabricated out of old hoops, or any other bits of iron which it was found practicable to gather in from a thousand different sources. This done, the recruits were trained to wield their weapons in a rude but not inefficient way; and having places assigned to them along the ramparts, presented when arranged there a very formidable appearance. They declared themselves willing to die at their posts, whenever the necessity might arise.

Meanwhile, that as far as was possible the hazard of famine might be provided against, foraging parties went forth on two successive days, and brought back with them one hundred and seventy head of cattle, with between six and seven hundred sheep.

The cattle were slaughtered at once, and salted down, for there was no fodder on which to support them; and the sheep were sent out every morning to graze upon the marshes that intervened between the river and the town wall, shepherds and an armed covering party attending them. And finally, every tree and bush within sight of the place was cut down, and all the doors and timber-work from the houses near were carried off and laid up as winter fuel. This done, men drew their breath with increased facility, and received with indifference the contradictory rumours, now of coming assaults, now of relief at hand, which from day to day, and well nigh from hour to hour, poured in upon them.

I have had occasion to speak of the mechanical genius of Lieut. Sinclair of the 13th Light Infantry, and of the manner in which he exercised his talent to promote the hilarity of his comrades during the peaceful occupation of Cabul. In Jellalabad a more important field of usefulness was afforded to him. There was not a mill in the place, and hence the corn which the foragers brought in, however acceptable it might be to the horses, could not by the men of the garrison be converted into bread. Mr. Sinclair took the matter up, and in due time produced as many hand-mills as sufficed to grind from day to day the quantity of flour that was required. It is unnecessary to add that if, while prosecuting his work, the gallant mechanic found both amusement and occupation, its completion was hailed with extreme delight by his brother soldiers. Cakes baked upon the coals, or cooked over heated stones, now took the place of parched corn, and the change was felt by all to whom it applied as a serious improvement in their physical condition.

Dr. Brydon recovered; so did the sergeant-major of the 37th Native Infantry, who had declined returning with the money bearers to Lughman; but an unfortunate Greek merchant, who had escaped the slaughter of Koord Cabul and Gundamuck, died of lock-jaw brought on by excessive suffering: he was buried in one of the ditches. Neither did the gallant garrison forget, amid the difficulties of its situation, to pay the customary honours to such days of fête as occurred. On the 12th of February a royal salute was fired in honour of the Prince of Wales's birthday, which caused no slight sensation when first the roar of the artillery was heard,—they who were not in the secret coming hastily to the conclusion that General Pollock with his army was in sight : for it is due to Lord Auckland's administration to record, that no sooner did intelligence of the state of things in Afghanistan reach them, than they despatched Pollock to take the command of the corps which was to carry relief to the forces in Cabul. And Pollock's arrival in Peshawur having already been ascertained, people naturally looked for his appearance in the valley of Jellalabad from one day to another. Pollock, however, did not come, but instead of him, the white tents of Akbar Khan were seen on the morning of the 15th on the farther side of the river, and about six miles distant from the walls ; and, as rumour had been very busy for some days previously, describing both the force which he commanded and the desperate intentions by which he was actuated, the near prospect of a struggle, on the issue of which their lives must depend, became manifest to the garrison, and was greeted cheerfully.

Hard and steadily the men laboured in the ditches and on the ramparts round about. They were merry, too, at their tasks, for the officers shared them ; and, all faring alike, there sprang up between these classes that sort of companionship which in well-regulated corps always exists near an enemy, and which, so far from relaxing, tightens, while it renders easy to be borne, the bonds of discipline. They had worked, moreover, to such an excellent purpose, especially during the 16th, 17th, and 18th, that the acting engineer began to consider how far it might be necessary to keep them so many hours in each day to their tasks. But while on the 19th he was pondering this matter, and giving directions that the scarp of the ditch should be polished off, an event befel, so sudden and so awful, that to his dying day none who witnessed will ever be able to forget it.

The morning of the 19th set in cold and windy. It was perhaps as comfortless an opening to the day as had been experienced since the occupation of the town ; yet there were no manifestations in the sky or in the state of the atmosphere of any storm brewing. Accordingly the men marched out as usual, carrying their arms with them ; and having piled the latter, took spade and pickaxe in hand, and plied them cheer-

L

fully. The guards were, as usual, at the gates; the sentries
occupied their accustomed posts along the ramparts; and the
officers not on duty sought amusement in walking or riding,
some outside the walls, others within the circle of the lines.
Col. Monteith, who happened to be field-officer for the day, had
ascended one of the bastions, and was sweeping the horizon with
his telescope, when all at once the earth began to tremble, and
there was a noise, not so much like thunder as of a thousand
heavily-laden waggons rolling and jolting over an ill-paved
street. The effect upon all over whom the spell of the pheno-
menon was cast is not to be described. They looked up and
around them with a stare of consternation; and then, as if actuated by one common influence, the parties in the trenches,
seizing their arms, rushed out. It was well for them that they
did so; for scarcely had they reached the glacis ere the whole
of the plain began to heave like billows on the surface of the
ocean, and walls and houses, splitting asunder, came tumbling
down upon the space which but an instant before had been
crowded with workmen. No man who saw that sight could any
longer be at a loss to realise the " opening by the earth of its
mouth, and the swallowing of Dathan and Abiram and their
household;" for the earth did open her mouth and close it repeatedly, receiving on one occasion into the horrid gulf an
officer high in rank and throwing him forth again, happily without the infliction on his person of any serious damage.

The earthquake of the 19th of February undid in an hour all
that it had taken the garrison of Jellalabad three months to
accomplish. The whole of the parapets which had been with
so much skill and diligence constructed were thrown down with
a fearful crash into heaps of ruins. In the walls, breaches were
made, more accessible than any which the troops found when
they first entered the place; and the entire circuit was more or
less shaken. As to the houses in the town, there was scarcely
one of them which escaped more or less of damage. Some fell
in altogether; others had their fronts or flanks destroyed and
the roofs shaken down; and the cloud of dust which rose immediately on the occurrence of the catastrophe is described as
having been portentous. Happily, very few lives were lost.
By far the greater number of the troops, being without the

walls when the shock came, stood upon the glacis, or lay flat, while it heaved beneath them, to witness the overthrow; and the guards, making for open spaces, escaped. Some natives were overwhelmed in the ruins of the houses where they sojourned; and Colonel Monteith, before he could escape from the rampart, sustained some bruises. But, on the whole, the casualties were wonderfully rare; and the stores, both of ammunition and salted provisions, sustained no damage.

It is at moments like these, and amid such a convulsion of nature, that the sense of his own nothingness is forced upon the least considerate of men. Battle and the tempest at sea are in some sort familiar both to soldiers and sailors; and if the occurrence of either sober them for the momemt, the impression soon wears off when the cause which immediately produced it has ceased to operate. But the earthquake, and especially such an earthquake as this, speaks to their moral nature in a sterner tone, and awakens in them emotions which do not pass away in an hour. I could, if delicacy did not forbid the proceeding, specify more than one instance wherein the effect of the convulsion of that day was to stir for the first time the religious principle in bosoms which had never before acknowledged it. At the same time none could look round upon the havoc that had occurred without feeling that the place, with all its inmates, was as open to the assault of the enemy as it had ever been since the brigade took possession of it. Indeed, circumstances were so much less favourable now than formerly, that the armed strength of Afghanistan was free to be carried whithersoever Akbar Khan might direct; and his desire to make himself master of the town was too openly expressed to admit of a doubt regarding his application of it to that purpose. Now, as his army stood scarce six miles from the glacis, it was impossible to imagine that he would long remain in ignorance of the havoc which had been wrought in the defences. What was to be done? That point the decision of the commander, and the excellent spirit that pervaded the troops, decided at once. Throughout the 19th, whenever from time to time shocks, though less violent than the first, occurred, the garrison was satisfied to maintain an attitude of watchfulness; and at night all lay upon their arms, sleeping at their alarm-posts. But the dawn of the 20th found them once

more with spade and pickaxe in hand, clearing away the rubbish
and filling up the breaches as well as they could.   At the same
time Sir Robert Sale considered it expedient to despatch a hasty
messenger to Peshawur with a letter which contained a full
account of the catastrophe, and urged General Pollock to march
to their relief.   But General Pollock either did not receive the
despatch, or he found himself unable to comply with the requi-
sition which it contained; and the garrison was in consequence
left, as it had been before, to depend upon the care of Providence
and its own vigilance and exceeding gallantry.

CHAPTER XIX.

Siege continued—Sortie.

THERE was no falling away in the confidence of these brave men, nor any change in their manner of life, either with or without the lines. Anticipating a stricter investment, they made good use of the opportunities that were present with them ; and sending out daily grass-cutting and foraging parties, they did their best to provide a little stock of necessaries against the season of increased difficulty. As was to be expected, these forays were not invariably executed without loss. The enemy's cavalry, of which about two thousand were understood to be in camp, made occasional dashes where they imagined that the foragers were without support; and though always checked, and sometimes severely punished by the troopers of the 5th, they here and there inflicted a blow that was felt. On such occasions the guns on the bastions did excellent service. The whole country within long range of the walls had been carefully measured by the artillery officers, and certain marks set up by which the distance could be accurately calculated; and the consequence was, that every shot thrown where a group of Afghans presented themselves, told. Indeed, to such perfection was the gunnery of the place carried, that a man and horse at eight hundred or a thousand yards' distance ran extreme risk of being cut down by a round shot; and on one occasion, at least, Captain Backhouse struck down a cavalier who could not have approached within a mile of the fort.

No satisfactory reason has ever been assigned for the reluctance which Akbar Khan manifested to bring his dispute with the garrison of Jellalabad to the arbitrament of a hand-to-hand fight. Though the earthquake occurred on the 19th, and he could not but be aware of its effects upon the English works, Akbar kept up to the 26th his encamping ground on the Cabul side of the river. Then, however, he put his people in motion, and about an hour before noon large masses of men were seen approaching, who, throwing themselves round the place, took possession of the whole circle of remote forts and heights, and rendered the blockade, to all outward appearance, complete. Parties were then pushed forward, which, getting under cover of some broken walls about five hundred yards from the southern part of the town, opened a fire upon every thing which showed itself above the parapet. This continued throughout the whole day, the people on Piper's Hill fusillading in like manner; yet not a man nor animal of any kind sustained hurt. Meanwhile the British artillery made occasional answers to the best purpose. It was curious to see the round shot strike the loose stones, causing the men who had sought shelter behind them to flee in all directions; while the shell practice towards the Piper's Hill, judging from the commotion which it produced, must have been excellent. But not a musket was discharged; for in the scarcity of musket ammunition lay the main source of weakness in Jellalabad; and because it was considered unwise to expose them to insult which they could not repel, the infantry, much to their own regret, were kept on the alert under arms, indeed, but within the city walls.

In this manner February wore away. Repeated shocks of earthquake, though in a milder form than those of the 19th, marked its progress, and it was as prolific as its predecessors had been in rumours of all kinds. But it produced no event of which, because of its influence on the fate of the campaign, it is worth while to make mention. The same sort of annoyance which he had given to the garrison on the 28th, Akbar renewed to as little purpose on the 2nd of March, till towards the evening, when a party of sappers sallied forth, and drove the Afghan skirmishers away.

The 3rd of March was a season of comparative repose. The enemy did not approach the walls, having suffered for their temerity, in this respect, the previous day; but on the 4th a great movement was seen in their camp, and the garrison stood at once to its arms. Large bodies of men moved round the northern face of the town, and took up a position in a grove, about a mile and a half in the direction of Peshawur. It was calculated by those who watched the proceeding through their telescopes, that the force collected there could not fall short of a thousand infantry and five hundred horse. Neither was there any mistake as to the design of the manœuvre. Akbar, distrusting his power of carrying the place by assault, was resolved to reduce it by famine, and the grove was occupied as affording a convenient point whence attacks might be made on the foraging parties when they went out; while all communication with the district which had heretofore sent in the chief portion of the supplies was cut off. Akbar had not reckoned, however, on the skill of the artillerists that lay behind the walls; neither, in all probability, was he aware that to a more remote circumference the radii of the circle, of which Jellalabad was the centre, had all been accurately measured. Wherefore, the whole of his plan suffered interruption the moment the battery on the south-east bastion opened, for every shot struck into the midst of his people; and after the fourth had told, the division retired in confusion to a more remote camping ground.

Meanwhile, from morning till night, strong working-parties plied their intrenching tools. They were not permitted to do so unmolested, for clouds of Afghans crept up under cover wherever they could find it, and fired long shots incessantly, though not to much purpose. At length the officers devised a scheme for drawing off this fire from the men, which proved for a time eminently successful, and occasioned great mirth in the garrison. They dressed up a wooden image, and put a cocked hat on its head, painting the face so as to make it resemble, when seen from a distance, an officer of rank, and raising it from time to time above the parapet, drew such a storm of fire towards it, as left the working-party free. They would cause it to move backwards and forwards, likewise, as if the General had been reconnoitring, and occasionally let it fall, whereupon a loud shout from the Afghan skirmishers gave indication that they were amazingly pleased with themselves. It is scarcely necessary to add, that the enemy's shout was responded to by peals of laughter from the garrison; but the trick seemed to be discovered at last, and then the effigy was removed.

In this manner things went on from one day to another. The enemy received continual reinforcements, while the garrison was thrown more and more upon its own resources; and to add to

the boldness of the one, and the difficulties in the position of
the other, every hour brought tidings of defeat and disaster to
the English arms elsewhere. At Cabul matters were almost as
desperate as they could be. The Shah, shut up in the Balla
Hissar, could scarcely hold his ground ; while Colonel Palmer,
who, with a regiment of Native Infantry had kept Ghuznee till
famine stared him in the face, was reported to have capitulated.
No man's heart, however, failed him, of all Sale's gallant band,
because of these things ; on the contrary, they felt that there was
the greater need for them to retain their hold upon the country :
and, perceiving that the assailants were becoming more daring
than heretofore, Sale determined to read them a lesson, as he had
formerly done. It was observed on the morning of the 10th,
that the enemy had been busy over-night, for the dawn of day
showed a number of songas, or stout breast-works, thrown up
within two hundred yards of the ditch, and that each was lined
with its armed party became manifest from the heavy musketry fire
that was poured from them all. Moreover, some spies reported
that Akbar had begun to mine, and that he was running his
chamber under a part of the wall, which having been blown up
during a former siege, had led to the capture of the place. A
rumour of this sort was too serious to be treated with neglect ;
wherefore, orders were issued for a portion of the brigade to make
ready for a sortie on the morrow, and Colonel Dennie was warned
to take the command, and to direct the movement.

At dawn of day on the 11th of March, three hundred men of
the 13th, as many of the 35th Native Infantry, with two hundred
sappers and miners, having Captain Broadfoot at their head,
marched out of the Peshawur gate. At the same time the whole
of the cavalry passed through the south gate, and formed in the
plain ; while the artillery, manning their guns on the ramparts,
opened such a fire upon the songas as rendered it exceedingly
inconvenient for anybody to show his head above them. There
was a great stir in Akbar's camp. His whole army, horse and
foot, turned out with much alacrity ; and the former made more
than one attempt to march forward—but so destructive was the
cannonade from the walls, that they never got beyond a certain
line, ere they broke and fled. Meanwhile the British infantry,
throwing out skirmishers, pressed on ; and driving the enemy's

advanced posts before them, soon forced their way to the breast-
works, and knocked them to pieces. It was ascertained at the
same time, beyond the possibility of doubt, that no attempt at
mining had been made: and the purpose of the sally having thus
been effected, Colonel Dennie caused the bugles to sound the
recall. According to custom in such cases, the British troops
no sooner began to fall back, than the enemy trod boldly upon
their footsteps. The skirmish became, therefore, more warm
than ever, and Captain Broadfoot, who with his sappers bore the
brunt of it, received a musket-ball through the thigh. But the
moment our people halted, and formed as if to charge, the
Afghans fled in confusion! The result of the operation was a
few casualties on the side of the garrison, without the loss of a
single life: while of the enemy about a hundred were supposed
to have fallen; and the sprinkling of dead bodies over the field
of battle was considerable.

It were tedious to tell how, day by day, events similar to those
which have already been described came to pass. The enemy,
though worsted in every skirmish, relaxed nothing in their boldness; but took up again the ground which they had lost, as soon
as our people withdrew from it. Their breast-works, in like
manner, sprang up after they had been thrown down, with marvellous celerity; while their fire was as constant, as teasing, and
in the main as harmless, as it had been from the beginning.
Occasionally a ball would take effect; and once a sentinel was
killed, being shot through the loop-hole which enabled him to
look abroad in comparative security. Moreover, the musket
ammunition within the walls became so scarce, that instructions
were given to collect the bullets which the enemy threw, and to
run them into moulds for the use of the garrison. Some idea,
likewise, may be formed of the nature of the leaden hail under
which the garrison lived, when it is stated that one officer collected in a day for his own use not fewer than one hundred and
thirty bullets; and as powder was happily abundant, a supply of
cartridges came into store—not before it was needed. And here
it may be well to observe, that among the officers in garrison
there were many who had brought rifles and fowling-pieces to
the seat of war. These, for the lack of other game, took to prac-
tising against the Afghans; and many a capital shot was made,

not in wantonness, but always when the necessity for it arose.
For example, the grass-cutters went forth every morning to
collect fodder for the animals. If it was meant that they should
penetrate to a spot far removed from the walls, an armed party
escorted them ; if there seemed to be forage enough near at hand,
they were permitted to go unguarded, the sentinels on the ramparts looking out for them. On these occasions it was that the
good aim of one or more amateur riflemen saved many a valuable
life, and secured food for the cavalry horses ; for it was considered a mere amusement to keep an eye upon the enemy's
parties, and to knock down the boldest, as often as, in the attempt
to cut off the foragers, they ventured within range.

Meanwhile there was no end to the rumours which, partly by
means of spies, and partly through the exertions of messengers—
who, in consideration of large bribes, made their way beyond
the enemy's lines—reached the garrison. It was communicated
to Sir Robert Sale to-day, that General Pollock had begun his
march ; and two days afterwards the statement was contradicted
upon the very best authority. By and by, tidings of an attempt
having been made on Akbar Khan's life came in, which proved
to be substantially correct—for one of his people wounded him,
though, as further inquiry showed, the affair was the result of
accident. Letters, also, were received, at remote intervals,
from the prisoners at Lughman, which gave but an indifferent account of their condition and prospects, and occasioned
much sorrow to their friends. Moreover, warnings of an
assault arranged and about to be carried into effect were rife ;
and these met with the more ready credence, that in spite of the
defeats which they sustained in every skirmish, the enemy seemed
to grow continually bolder. Now they would show themselves
in force, manœuvre in their own way, and then disappear ; now
clouds of skirmishers would threaten the working-parties, and
force them to retire from the ditches within the walls. But a worse
evil than any of these threatened. Provisions began to fail.
Of grain, no further supplies had been received for weeks; and
the amount in store had become so scanty, that the fighting men
were put upon quarter allowance--the camp-followers denied
altogether. Meat, also, was grown very scarce. The salted
beef, which had been very carefully issued, was fast melting

away ; and not a hoof remained, either of cattle or of sheep.
Now it is comparatively a light thing to face armed men, provided you can rely upon the troops that serve under you ; but
when the means of feeding your own people begin to fail, your
situation, if you be in command of an army or a fortress, becomes
extremely distressing.   Sir Robert Sale, firm and gallant as he
was, felt this.   He therefore continued to bribe messenger after
messenger, whom he sent with instances more and more pressing,
to General Pollock at Peshawur.   But, though promises of
speedy relief were brought back in abundance, no prospect of
their fulfilment opened upon him ; and both he, and the noble
fellows who met him daily in his audience chamber, began, in
spite of themselves, to become both anxious and impatient.

CHAPTER XX.

Battle of the 7th of April—Fall of Colonel Dennie.

IT was now the 1st of April; and during a space of four months
and a half this handful of British troops had maintained itself
against disaster, against frequent attacks, against rumours of evil
on every side—in the heart of an enemy's country. Another and
still more terrible danger was beginning to threaten; and sickness, which is ever the forerunner of absolute famine, showed
itself among the camp-followers. The soldiers, to be sure, were
healthy to a degree that has no parallel in the history of warfare.
Not one suffered, except from wounds, and all were become as
hard as iron; for neither heat, nor cold, nor moisture, seemed to
produce the smallest effect upon them. Even the earthquake
had in some sort lost its terrors. It returned continually; and
once, at least, with such violence as to crack the walls which,
with so much labour, they had for the second time placed in a
defensible condition. Yet no man's heart failed him; and as
for service in sortie or foraging, all were ready for it at a
moment's notice. The practice in Jellalabad was this. Nobody
wore his uniform. Red coats closely buttoned up were found to
be very inconvenient garments for men who had to handle the
spade and the axe more frequently than the musket; so the
regimental clothing was all put in store, and fatigue jackets, or
perhaps no jackets at all, became the order of the day. Over
these, or else over their shirts, the men slung their accoutrements, and, with sleeves tucked up, laboured, in good spirits and
with exceeding industry, the officers digging beside them. Suddenly there would arise a cry that the enemy were approaching.
Down went spade and pickaxe, and forth from their places in the
pile the loaded muskets were plucked; and then up upon the
glacis, and away across the gardens and enclosures near it, these
gallant fellows ran, in the best of all skirmishing order. They
did not know what it was to sustain a repulse; and hence they

faced fearlessly, and bore down on all occasions any excess of numbers. If ever men had learned to consider themselves invincible, the garrison of Jellalabad, under their veteran leader, had achieved that end. And when troops become fairly convinced that it is impossible to beat them, the assailants who make the attempt, be they whom they may, will find that they have set themselves to a job of no ordinary toughness.

It was the 1st of April, and the grass-cutters having been out, as usual, early in the morning, were returned with a small supply of forage for the horses and beasts of burthen. The supply, however, was more scanty than heretofore. Indeed, for some time back the enemy had striven to cut off the garrison from this resource, by driving flocks of sheep upon the meadow-lands, and sending them, under an escort, as near as from four to six hundred yards from the crest of the glacis. To-day they repeated the manœuvre; and Sir Robert Sale determined to try whether it might not be possible to make them smart for it. With this view the cavalry were ordered to mount, without sound of trumpet; while six hundred and fifty infantry, namely, one hundred and fifty sappers, with two hundred from each of the regular regiments, got under arms, and made ready to support them. Suddenly the south gate was thrown open; and a part of the horse, crossing the drawbridge at speed, made for the sheep. No sooner were they seen than the shepherds ran to drive their flocks away; but the troopers were too quick for them. Having headed the nearest flock and secured it, they rode at another, and, heading them in like manner, cut down the shepherds ere they could escape. Meanwhile the rest of the cavalry, with the infantry supports, hurried on; and a body of grass-cutters, armed with poles, being thrown in rear of each flock, not fewer than three were driven towards the town.

There was great consternation, as may be imagined, in Akbar's camp, and an earnest desire to prevent, if possible, the besieged escaping with the prey. Multitudes of men, some on foot, others on horseback, turned out, and advanced at a rapid pace against the escort. But they soon found that the gunners on the ramparts had not forgotten their cunning. Shot after shot rushed through their masses, sweeping down whole sections; while the gallant 5th faced their horses round, and stood ready to meet, in mid-career, any force which might be induced to charge them. None, however, were bold enough to do so. And the consequence was that the sallying party returned into the town with the loss of one man killed, and a few wounded, driving not fewer than five hundred head of sheep before them.

Great was the joy of all concerned in this brilliant affair, and very hearty the congratulations that met them on their arrival; but of a still nobler trait in the character of the 35th Native Infantry I am bound to take notice, because it reminds me of the behaviour of Clive's sepoys at the celebrated defence of Arcot. On the 2nd Sir Robert Sale proceeded to distribute the captured sheep among the corps and departments composing his garrison. The 35th declined to accept the boon. They sent a deputation to the general, which respectfully acquainted him that animal food was less necessary for them than for Europeans, and besought him to give their portion of the booty to their gallant comrades of the 13th. No wonder that between these two corps there should have sprung up a romantic friendship, which, though the accidents of service have parted them, probably for ever, neither is likely to forget, at all events as a tradition, while they keep their places respectively in the armies of the Queen and of the East India Company.

From this date up to the 6th all remained comparatively quiet in and around Cabul. The enemy, who for some time back had begun to entrench themselves, continued their labours as briskly as ever; and connected their fortified camp, which was interposed between the besieged and Peshawur, with a line of castles on either flank. The garrison, in like manner, added daily to the strength of their defences; and sent out foraging parties, which sometimes succeeded, sometimes failed, in collecting supplies, and more than once sustained a sharp encounter while so employed. Meanwhile reports of General Pollock's proceedings, each contradictory of the other, continued to be brought in; till there arose a feeling within the lines that he must have attempted the Khyber and failed. Indeed, a rumour to this effect became rife on the evening of the 5th; and when, on the following day, the thunder of Akbar's guns was heard firing a salute, that which had previously amounted only to suspicion grew into something like conviction. And now came the question, What was to be

done? Five hundred mountain sheep soon pass away, where there
are two thousand mouths to be fed with them; and mutton alone,
if bread or rice be wanting, ceases by degrees to be palatable. A
council of war was accordingly summoned, to which the plan of
a general attack on the enemy's position was proposed. It was
shown that ammunition, not less than food, would soon become
scarce; and the point was started whether, assuming that Pollock
had sustained a repulse, it would not be better to cut a way
through the enemy's lines than to abide where they were, till
either famine or the want of means wherewith to defend themselves should compel a surrender. There were not two opinions
in that council. All voted for the nobler proceeding; and each,
as he gave his opinion, fortified it by reminding his friends, that
if they must perish, it would be better to die like men, with arms
in their hands. For the memory of the slaughter in Koord Cabul
was yet fresh with them; and they were not so simple as to
believe that, in the event of an entrance within their works being
effected, they would fare better at the hands of an exasperated foe
than their comrades had done. Wherefore orders were given to
pack up everything; baggage, stores, ammunition, all that they
had; and to keep it in readiness to move, under a proper guard,
as soon as the way should have been cleared for such a convoy
by success in a great battle.

Men lay down that night in a graver frame of mind than usual.
There was no distrust about them, none whatever. They had
the same confidence in their leader and in themselves that they
ever had, and hoped, as heretofore, for victory. But if the
terms in which they committed themselves to the protection
of a higher power were more solemn, perhaps deeper, than any
which on former occasions had been used, the reader who thinks
at all will be little surprised at the circumstance. They were
about to throw their last die. They were going to engage in their
final battle; for, let it terminate how it might, there would not
remain for them musket ammunition enough to try the fortune
of another. It was necessary, therefore, that their victory should
be, not only sure, but complete; so complete as to open for them
a free passage to the head of the Khyber—perhaps beyond it.
And as they knew that the force opposed to them, besides being
well supplied with guns from Cabul, could not number less than

nine thousand fighting men, it is not to be wondered at if they
looked forward to the business of the morrow with solemnity.
But when the stir began, when, rising without sound of bugle or
beat of drum, they took their places in the ranks—three columns,
parallel, and each facing the gate through which it was to pass—
they all felt that their nerves were strung magnificently, and that
each would do his duty.   And, one and all, they did it.

The order of battle on the memorable 7th of April was this:—
The whole of the infantry, consisting of the 13th and 35th, with
350 sappers, formed into three columns of attack.   They severally consisted of pretty nearly the same numerical strength;
for to the sappers one company from the 13th, and another from
the 35th, were added : and they mustered each about five hundred
bayonets.   Twelve men alone were left as a guard at each of the
city gates ; and the walls were manned by the camp followers.
Moreover, there had been lowered from the ramparts, in the
course of the previous afternoon, six nine-pounders, of which
Captain Abbott now took the command ; and these being well
horsed, prepared to push forward in the interval between the
left and the centre columns.   Finally, the cavalry, as usual, were
ready for their work ; and the different commands having been
settled—Monteith with his own regiment, Dennie with his, and
Captain Havelock of the 13th being put in charge of the third
—the whole set forward with a firm pace, a due proportion of
skirmishers covering them.

Between the Afghan entrenched camp and Jellalabad there
were two or three forts, which the enemy occupied in strength,
and which constituted their advanced posts.   It had been agreed
that the columns should pass them by ; and making straight for
the lines, accomplish the overthrow of the main body in the first
instance, and then return to the attack, should the garrisons
continue to hold them.   But a flanking fire from one of these
told so severely upon the 13th Light Infantry, that Sir Robert Sale
suddenly commanded it to bring forward the left shoulder, and
fall upon the place by a breach which seemed to be practicable.
With undaunted resolution the 13th rushed at the fort, Colonel
Dennie nobly leading ; and finding the aperture sufficiently large
to admit of it, they rushed through the outer wall—only to find
themselves exposed to a murderous fire from the untouched de-

fences of the inner keep.   Here Dennie received, just as he approached the breach, his mortal wound.   A ball entered the side,
passing through the sword-belt; and he bent forward upon his
horse.   Lieut. and Adjutant (now Captain) Wood instantly rode
up to him, and expressed a hope that the hurt was not serious.
But it was more than serious; it was fatal.   A couple of orderlies,
by Captain Wood's direction, turned his horse's head homewards,
and leading it by the bridle, endeavoured to guide him to the
town.   But he never reached it alive.   He died with the sound
of battle in his ears, hoping, but not living to be assured, that it
would end triumphantly.

So fell as brave a soldier as the British army ever produced,
and as good an officer as served throughout the war in Afghanistan.   There would have been great lamentation over him had
the hurry and excitement of the fight permitted those who took
part in it to divert their thoughts from the business that was immediately before them.   But soldiers when engaged with the
enemy have no time to indulge the finer feelings; and the gallant
13th found themselves already in such a position as bent all
their care, and that of their leaders, towards finding the best and
readiest method of extrication from it.   The inner tower or keep
it was manifest could not be carried.   There was no breach,
nor any means of ingress, except through a doorway elevated to half the height of the tower; and as the ladder by
which alone it could be approached was removed, the men, however willing to force an entrance one by one, could not reach the
threshold.   After a brief pause, therefore, the word was given
to pass on, and emerge into the open plain through an aperture
on the further side; and then the original plan, the deviation
from which had effected no good, was resumed.   On they went,
at the double—driving before them the skirmishers which made a
show of resistance, till they gained the entrenchments, and broke
through with a loud shout.   Meanwhile both Colonel Monteith's
and Captain Havelock's columns had trodden down all opposition.
The former maintained, without a check, the pace at which their
advance began.   The latter, sweeping round by the river in
order to turn the flank of the position, became exposed to the
attack of the enemy's cavalry; and were more than once obliged
to form square, which they did with the precision of an ordinary

M

field-day. But they too gained their point : and now the three divisions uniting, poured such a fire upon the enemy's masses, as dissolved them quite. Their guns, which had been served with much boldness, were in consequence deserted. One they endeavoured to carry away with them, but a well directed round shot from Abbott's battery killed both of the horses which had just been harnessed to the limber; after which the rout became universal. Had the force of British cavalry been such as could have been launched, without support, in pursuit, few would have escaped to tell the tale of that day's overthrow. As it was, the fugitives being chased towards the river, rushed madly in, and perished, almost as many amid the deep water as by the bayonets and shot of the pursuers.

Never was victory more complete. Camp, baggage, artillery, ammunition, standards, horses, arms of every kind, fell into the hands of the conquerors. The camp they committed to the flames; of the baggage, as well as of animals to transport it, they conveyed back to Jellalabad as much as they cared to preserve ; and were specially gratified by discovering in one of the forts that flanked the lines, an important magazine of powder, shells, and shot. All these they carried with exceeding joy to the town, where in the course of a very few hours provisions became abundant : for the fame of the battle and of its results soon spread abroad ; and as Akbar with the wreck of his army fled towards Cabul, all the chiefs of districts in the other direction hastened to send in their submission.

CHAPTER XXI.

Arrival of Pollock's Army—Great sickness and suffering.

THE action of the 7th of April may be said to have decided the fate of Jellalabad and its " illustrious garrison." Single-handed they broke the power of him under whom the main army of occupation had fallen; and were in a condition either to keep the ground for many months longer, or to force their way back to the provinces at will. For obvious reasons, Sir Robert Sale determined to persevere in the course which he had hitherto followed. Having retained his hold of the country so long and so tenaciously, he would not relinquish it now, especially since he ascertained that General Pollock had suffered no defeat in the Khyber, but was, on the contrary, winning his way through, though not without some loss, and a good deal of difficulty. Accordingly, a market was opened outside one of the gates, to which the country people were encouraged to bring grain, and food of every kind. They were not exorbitant in their charges, for it was their object as well as that of their chiefs to conciliate the Feringhees now they had again won the ascendant; and the barefaced assurance with which many professed friendship, who, only a fortnight previously, had been in arms against the place, amused much more than it provoked the victors. One scoundrel, in particular, the same Guffoor Khan who had first trafficked with Sale, and then sought to betray him, became once more the most forward of his friends; and was treated with a degree of forbearance which, however honourable to the sagacity of the Brigadier, was very little in agreement with either the duplicity or the impudence of the Afghan.

Time passed, and every new day brought some tidings with it more or less to be depended upon. On the 10th the relieving army was heard of as having arrived at the middle of the Khyber. On the 14th letters came in to say that the difficulties of the pass

M 2

were all surmounted, and that the loss sustained in various
actions did not exceed one officer killed, two or three wounded,
and about one hundred and thirty-five men killed and wounded.
There was, of course, a feeling of satisfaction in the place, at
the near prospect of a junction with their friends. But mixed
with it there could not fail to be a proud sense of triumph likewise, for they should meet the comers now, not as men meet
those who deliver them from mortal danger, but as conquerors
welcoming to the scene of their triumphs comrades who have
arrived too late to share either the peril and the glory. And as
if to remove all doubts on that head, several officers, having obtained leave, set out by twos and threes, to visit Pollock's camp,
being yet a great way off. These confirmed by their appearance
the reports of the late victory, which were already in circulation
through the lines; and spoke of the facility with which the
march on Cabul might be executed, and the tarnished honour of
the British name retrieved. But they spoke to men on whose
minds the tale of the disasters of the previous year had made an
impression more deep, perhaps, than the occasion required.
General Pollock had formed his own plans, and was not to be
drawn away from them by the enthusiastic conversation of young
men flushed with recent successes. And so it came to pass, that
he neither quickened his progress to Jellalabad, nor spoke of
passing beyond it till means of transport should reach him more
abundant than he then possessed, or expected to be able to procure, in a province which for six long months and more had
been the theatre of a desperate and unceasing warfare.

The 15th of April brought Pollock's column within seven
miles of the lately beleaguered city. There it halted, at a
place called Alee Bogham, and encamped for the night. Many
visitors from the city flocked to welcome the new comers; and
on the following day the band of the 13th went forth to meet
them. There was a hearty cheer on both sides; after which the
musicians facing about began, according to immemorial usage,
to play the strangers in. I do not know whether some touch of
waggery might have prompted the choice of the air, yet when
the band struck up a Jacobite melody—beautiful in itself, and
full of meaning—all who heard acknowledged its fitness to the
occasion. The relieving force marched the last two or three

CHAP. XXI.] JUNCTION WITH GENERAL POLLOCK.	165

miles towards Jellalabad to the cadence of " Oh, but ye 've been lang o' coming ! "

The tale of the siege and defence of Jellalabad is told. Relief came at last, after the garrison, by its own prowess, had dispersed the investing force; and hearty congratulations were exchanged between the brave who came to succour, and the brave who had fought their own battle. It seemed, also, to the wondering marchers that the tales which had been told them of suffering and danger in the place must have been mere inventions. Never had they looked upon troops in higher condition or better order: the very clothing of these men seemed as if it had just come out of store—no soil nor stain being upon its brightness; and their belts and accoutrements were as clean as if for the last half year they had had no more important business to attend to than to keep them so. And as to their countenances, bronzed they unquestionably were through continual exposure to the weather, but not one among them all gave token of other than the rudest health. Moreover, there was food in abundance for their visitors as well as for themselves, and freely they dispensed it. That evening the officers of the garrison entertained at dinner as many of their comrades as were not required for duty; and the latter bringing wine and other luxuries in their train, the entertainment went off with great éclat.

From this date the proceedings of Sale's brigade so completely blend and fall in with the operations of General Pollock's army that to continue the narrative of the one, as from day to day events occurred, would involve the necessity of entering into a minute detail of the other. The latter task has, however, been so fully performed by those who have written about operations in which they were personally engaged, that to go beyond a summary on the present occasion would be out of place. I content myself, therefore, with borrowing the substance of a journal which seems to have been kept with diligence and care by an officer of the 13th Light Infantry; and which, therefore, traces accurately the various movements and services of the brigade of which I have in some sort become the historian.

Though the rearmost of Pollock's regiments closed up and gathered about Jellalabad so early as the first week in May,

August had well nigh run itself out ere the campaign can
be said to have opened.   All this while the troops lay encamped upon a sandy plain, where there was no shelter from
the burning rays of the sun; where forage for the cattle was
exceedingly scarce; provisions for the men hard to be got;
wine, tea, brandy, and other luxuries, all but unattainable, and
the water itself neither agreeable nor salubrious. Sickness,
as might have been anticipated, soon began to show itself; and
day by day people died of dysentery and fever. Horses and
camels perished in like manner; and as the latter were not very
carefully put under ground, the stench from their putrifying
carcases soon became intolerable. The odours which in a tropical climate float upon the atmosphere of a camp are anything
but agreeable at the best; and if to these be added the effluvium
that arises from decaying animal matter, pestilence is sure to
follow. Moreover, the flies come in myriads, and there, in Jellalabad, and over the face of the country round it, they absolutely swarmed. The very air became black with them; and
they entered into men's food, and crawled over their persons,
polluting whatever they touched. It was a season of intense
suffering to the troops, that during which they seemed to rest
upon their oars. For the town became a perfect Lazar-house.
The camp was little better; and the sufferers from a burning
heat sought shelter against it by digging holes in the ground and
sleeping in them at the hazard of being buried alive, as in one
instance, at least, actually befel.

For this inaction, and the consequences arising out of it,
General Pollock was not to blame. He acted under orders that
were distinct and peremptory; and found himself besides so deficient in baggage animals, that to wield the power of which he
was possessed became impossible. It seemed, too, as if the remembrance of recent disasters had paralysed the energies of the
supreme government at Calcutta. With a change of rulers a
change of policy took place. It was natural that it should;
neither can it be wondered at if they, on whom the responsibility
now rested, shrank from the prospect of risking a second
army where the first had perished. But negotiation, which the
General had been directed to try, was soon shown to be pro-
fitless. Akbar Khan refused to liberate his prisoners; and

having put down the remains of Shah Shujah's party, exercised supreme authority in his father's name.

So passed the months of May and June—amid sickness and much suffering, the necessary results in almost all cases of inactivity when an army is in the field. One event occurred, indeed, to interrupt the monotony of existence, and in its way it was a curious one. There arrived in July at Jellalabad a body of Seikh troops, consisting both of infantry and cavalry, to the amount of perhaps five thousand five hundred men. They were stout fellows, and well armed, marching in good order, and keeping their ranks at a halt; but, except as regarded their drill, they seemed to be under no effective discipline whatever. Two months' pay was issued to them a few days after their arrival, which, so far from mollifying or humanising them, produced an effect diametrically the reverse: they began forthwith to quarrel among themselves, and fighting it out with muskets and ball cartridges mutually gave and received much damage. About a dozen men were killed, and some hundreds wounded ere the fray could be stopped. Nor did the matter end there. A body of about two hundred horse rose upon their commandant, put him to death, burned his tents, and, mounting their bony half-starved looking steeds, rode back to Peshawur. The only cause which they assigned for the mutiny was disgust at being kept idle instead of going where plunder, and the gratification of a bitter hatred of the Afghans—on both of which they had counted—might be obtained.

Meanwhile the "illustrious garrison," which had gone through the perils and restraints of a six months' siege without one hour of sickness, began to droop and languish. The hospitals became crowded; and even they who walked about and did their duty, looked feeble and ghastly. Under these circumstances General Pollock determined to try the effect upon them of a change of air and scene; and as he had at length received instructions to operate, either in advance or retreat, according to his own discretion, he made up his mind to move forward as soon as the means of conveyance would at all permit. Accordingly, on the 6th of August, Sale was directed with the 13th and 35th regiments, a troop of horse artillery, Broadfoot's sappers, and Tait's irregular horse, to march as far as Futtehabad,

on the road to Cabul. Now Futtehabad is distant from Jellalabad not more than seventeen miles; yet such was the en-
feebled condition of the troops that three days were required to
reach it. The first day the brigade marched only nine miles;
yet the gallant 13th left upwards of thirty stragglers behind; of
whom four died of apoplexy, two hours after they had been
removed to the hospital tent. The next day the column compassed only four miles, and suffered severely even during that
short stage; the third carried them to Futtehabad. It was
entirely deserted by its inhabitants, for, having made themselves
conspicuous by the butchery of some helpless fugitives from
General Elphinstone's corps, they not unnaturally expected that
a terrible punishment awaited them. Neither did they wholly
escape. Every house in the place was rased to the ground; the
gardens and orchards were laid waste, and the trees cut down;
after which the men pitched their tents, and in a place where
forage was abundant, and air and water were alike pure, they
picked up from day to day that vigour both of body and mind
which a little longer sojourn in Jellalabad would have destroyed
beyond the possibility of redemption.

For three weeks Sale and his brigade enjoyed a monopoly of
their agreeable encamping ground. They were not altogether
weeks of inaction; for Sale was one of those fiery spirits which,
if there be anything to be done, cannot rest till it has been accomplished; and being informed of a design on Akbar Khan's
part to occupy with a body of riflemen a fort distant from Futtehabad about seven miles, he resolved to anticipate the proceeding. With this view, three hundred men of the 35th Native
Infantry, two guns, and two hundred of Tait's horse, were added
to Captain Broadfoot's sappers; and the whole were directed to
proceed, under Broadfoot's orders, to the fort in question, and
to destroy it. There was some little show of resistance at first,
which would have been vigorously conducted had Akbar's riflemen been there; but Broadfoot had got the start of the Jezalchies, and no sooner unlimbered his cannon than the people
behind the walls hung out a white flag. The place was immediately occupied, and sufficient powder being sent on under an
escort, the same evening the gate, with two of the bastions, were
mined and blown up. Then followed a course of devastation,

of which, though it may have been necessary for the purpose of striking terror elsewhere, we cannot, now that all angry feeling has subsided, read without regret. The castle was one of Akbar Khan's favourite summer residences. It was surrounded by orchards of fruit-trees, and the village that had sprung up beneath the shelter of its bulwarks lay in the heart of a succession of gardens. Every house was destroyed, every tree barked or cut down; after which, the detachment having collected a considerable spoil of bullocks, sheep, and goats, marched back to camp.

Scarcely was this feat performed ere letters announced to Sir Robert Sale that the whole army was on the eve of breaking up its camp and marching upon Cabul. The news was welcomed both by the Brigadier and his followers with hearty good will; for the number of sick in hospital had diminished one half, and the convalescents were already fit for duty: and when on the 16th the 3rd Light Dragoons, together with a second troop of horse artillery, joined, hope appeared to grow into assurance. Nor did many days elapse ere tokens more explicit of a campaign fairly begun appeared. A proclamation signed by General Pollock was circulated far and wide, and sent in by spies and hired messengers to Cabul. It informed the people of the country that a British army was again about to occupy the capital, and warned those to whom the safe keeping of the British prisoners might have been intrusted, that any act of cruelty or wrong perpetrated upon these unfortunate persons, would draw down a signal revenge. The inhabitants of Cabul in particular were told that General Pollock expected to find his countrymen in that city, and that if any attempt were made to carry them off into the mountain districts, it would be at the peril of those who engaged in it. Nor, in truth, were either of these proclamations uncalled for. To Akbar Khan himself it is due to state that he seems to have acted with great kindness and delicacy towards the British subjects that had fallen into his hands. He refused, indeed, either to ransom or set them free, and carried them about from place to place, sometimes at a rate of travelling more rapid than was altogether compatible either with their habits or their convenience; but as far as his means extended, he supplied their wants with a liberal hand, and was invariably polite, and sometimes considerate, especially to the ladies. It

was not so with such chiefs of villages, especially among the Ghilzies, as managed to keep the prisoners whom they had secured
to themselves.   They were always harsh, and not unfrequently
cruel, especially to the sepoys and Hindostanee followers,
whom they seem to have regarded with an absolute hatred.   The
following may be taken as a specimen of the atrocities of which
these savage men were sometimes guilty.

An unfortunate Hindostanee had fallen into the hands of a
Ghilzee chief, whose village was not far removed from the British camp at Futtehabad.   The poor man, as soon as he learned
that his friends were in the neighbourhood, made, naturally
enough, an attempt to escape to them; but in this he was not
successful, for being overtaken he was brought back and carried
before the chief.   The latter upbraided him as if he had committed a crime, and, ordering him to be thrown down and held
upon the ground, exclaimed, " What! you want to go to the Feringhees, do you?"   So saying, the ruffian drew his heavy knife,
and with two blows cut off the wretched Hindoo's feet.   " Now,"
he cried, as the poor fellow lay in his blood, " you may go where
you will:" and the wounded man took him at his word.   He
crawled upon his hands and knees, after stanching the hemor-
rhage in some sort by tying strips of his turban round the
wounded limbs, and thus made his way into the British camp.
No one who reads this tale can be surprised to learn that a very
bitter feeling towards people who could perpetrate so frightful
an outrage pervaded the breasts of the soldiers of General Pollock's army, as well European as Native.

At length, on the 21st of August, the tide of war seemed
fairly to set in.   There arrived that day at Futtehabad Her
Majesty's 9th regiment of foot, two squadrons 10th Bengal
Cavalry, one squadron 5th cavalry, the 60th and 26th regiments
Native Infantry, with Abbott's battery of guns.   The commander-in-chief accompanied them in person; and on the following morning, leaving Sale's brigade behind, they pushed
forward towards Gundamuck.   They marched, likewise, as every
other corps in the army was directed to do, in the lightest possible order.   For the tents usually carried with an Indian force,
Sepoys' pauls, as the marquees of the native soldiers are styled,
were substituted.   The men's knapsacks, too, were emptied of

everything except a single change of linen, while the baggage of
the officers was cut down to the lowest, and they were required to
sleep three or four in the same marquee. Yet with all these
precautions, the means of transport proved in the hour of difficulty so inadequate that a much stronger garrison was left to
protect the rear than had been either contemplated or desired.
Moreover, not a man was permitted to go in advance of whom
it was even doubtful whether his physical powers would sustain
him.   All the sick, with most of the convalescents, were sent
back to Jellalabad.   In a word, the army was trimmed,
weeded, and fined down, till it consisted of not more than nine
or ten thousand troops, but they were excellent troops in regard
both to discipline and the strength and bravery of individuals;
and they were attended by five or six thousand Seikh soldiers,
besides about forty thousand followers.   As to the line of
camels, horses, ponies, bullocks, it seemed, when fairly set in
motion, to be interminable;—so unwieldy is an Asiatic host even
in the hands of Englishmen, so inveterate is the force of custom in a land where the climate both enervates the frame, and
induces tastes that agree but little with our European notions of
the proper bearing of a soldier.

CHAPTER XXII.

Advance of Pollock's Army to Cabul.

WHILE the British army thus prepared itself for a renewal of active operations, the voice of rumour described Akbar Khan as filled with alarm, and continually wavering in his counsels. To-day it was stated that, having put to death the last representative of the house of Shah Shujah, he had ascended the throne, and was resolved to maintain himself there to the last. To-morrow brought tidings of revolts and civil wars, of which the Prince Futteh Jung, after effecting his escape from Cabul, was the originator. A third report represented the son of Dost Mohammed as in full march towards Bameean, whence, carrying his prisoners along with him, he was prepared, on the first appearance of danger, to escape into Balkh. But that the nation was as little disposed as ever to bow the neck to a foreign yoke, all who spoke upon the subject seemed to be agreed. Hence, when towards the end of August the echoes of firing began to be heard in the passes, and the sky became illumined at night with the blaze of burning villages, none who listened to the sound, and gazed upon the spectacle, expressed the slightest surprise. For all men felt that they had the same game to play over again, which the more sanguine had regarded as brought to a close three years previously ; and a determination to play it better was universal in the ranks.

Wave after wave of the force which was to avenge the massacre of Elphinstone's corps moved on. The 21st brought Pollock with one division into Futtehabad ; the 22nd saw him push beyond it. On the 25th Brigadier Monteith came up, bringing with him Her Majesty's 31st regiment, the 33rd Native Infantry, the mountain-train, the 1st Light cavalry, and Ferreys's Jezalchies. By and by a smart action commenced upon the hills that overlook Mahmokan, which cost the English about fifty in killed and wounded, and resulted in the defeat of the enemy. And now, on the 2nd of September, Sale's brigade broke up; and after a night's rest at Heemlah, joined head-quarters on the 3rd at Gundamuck. Here a fresh distribution of the army took place. It was told off into two divisions, of one of which Sir Robert Sale was put in command; while the other was given in charge to General MacCaskill. But MacCaskill was at the time so much of an invalid that he could travel only in a litter; and Brigadier Monteith assumed in consequence the command, for which, both by nature and education, he was eminently fitted.

It is not my intention to trace the onward progress of General Pollock's army. The ground which it traversed was familiar to the members of the brigade, with the gallant deeds of which I am alone concerned; and from stage to stage there was sharp fighting. For the Ghilzies defended their mountains at every point which offered such a position as their manner of warfare required, and harassed front, main body, and rear, with a desultory fire from every precipice. At Jugdulluck there was a warm encounter; the enemy had fortified the top of the pass, and maintained themselves stoutly, till the 9th and 13th regiments mounted the hills on either flank, and drove them from their entrenchments. In the same manner, skirmishing all the way, the column proceeded by Kuttysung, Sey Baba, and Barrikab, to Tizeen, where a day's halt occurred for the purpose of enabling the rear to close up. And very harrowing to the feelings of the soldiers was this long march. The narrow path by which they moved was strewn with the remains of Elphinstone's army. One upon another lay the dead; some of them reduced to the condition of mere skeletons; others clothed, and with the features still so entire, that by many of their old acquaintances they were recognised. Flocks of vultures and other birds of prey wheeled over the heads of the living, and seemed to claim the dead as their own; while the smell that arose, especially on the night air, was dreadful. Our gallant fellows looked upon the scene of slaughter, and wished for revenge; and they never suffered an opportunity of gratifying the desire to pass unimproved.

There were some sharp affairs of posts at Tizeen, which ended invariably in the repulse of the enemy; nevertheless, the halt which it was found necessary to order here had the effect of increasing the confidence of the Ghilzies not a little. They appeared to imagine that, having got as far as this valley, the Feringhees distrusted their own power of penetrating beyond it. Wherefore Akbar Khan was sent for from a post which he had begun to fortify in the most difficult gorge of the Koord Cabul; and hastened with all his followers to join the array which the chiefs of Tizeen were drawing together. The position which they had chosen ran along the face and on the summits of the Huft Kothul. This is a cluster of mountains, seven in number, the highest of which rises to an elevation of nearly eight thousand feet above the level of the sea, and forms the ridge of that chain, which with various breaks may be said to extend all the way from Bootkak to Heemlah. The waters on either side run down in opposite directions; the road, which heretofore had been, except in the deep valleys, upon an ascent, changes, so as henceforth to go downwards. Moreover, as has been shown at length, while tracing the march of Sir Robert Sale's brigade to Jellalabad, the valley of Tizeen is closed in the rear, not less than in front, by precipitous rocks: wherefore the Afghans, assuming that the invaders had done their worst; that having penetrated thus far, they feared to go farther; not only assembled upon the Huft Kothul about fifteen thousand men, but threw a large body of men upon the rear of the valley, shutting up, as they imagined, their enemies in a trap. But they had miscalculated both the designs of the invaders and their own means of counteracting them; and in due time, after Pollock had assembled and re-freshed his troops, he proceeded to convince them of their error.

The road from Tizeen to Koord Cabul passes over a shoulder of the Huft Kothul. The leading column, consisting of the first division, traversed it under the ordinary protection of an advanced guard, and suffered no molestation till they approached the point where the pathway attains its extreme altitude; but here such a storm of fire assailed them that the air rang with the hissing of the bullets as they passed. In a moment, the 13th to the right, the 2nd Queen's to the left, spread in skirmishing order over the bases of the hills, and clambered up, returning the fire as they best could, yet scarcely appearing to check their onward progress, while they did so. The enemy fought with great des-peration, standing till but a few paces divided them from our troops ; and gave way even then only when the fixed bayonets gleamed before them, and they heard the shout wherewith the British infantry invariably preface a charge.   Then might be seen a flight and a pursuit, the one winged by terror, the other animated to perseverance by a burning thirst of revenge.   The 3rd Light Dragoons were let loose upon the fugitives.   They soon overtook them, and hewed, right and left, as men do who have the deaths of their friends and comrades to atone for ; and the whole summit of the hill, as well as the slope beyond it, and the road, and the declivities leading down to it, were strewed with the bodies of the slain.   Two pieces of artillery, both originally belonging to Elphinstone's corps, were taken here, and Akbar, routed to his heart's content, felt that he was indeed powerless.

The battle of Tizeen, as it was the sternest, so it was the last endeavour which the Afghans made to save the capital.   Not a shot was fired while the army, on the following day, threaded the frightful ravines of the Koord Cabul, doubly frightful now because of the heaps of dead bodies with which the narrow pathway was choked.   And when, after the halt of a night at Bootkak, the columns again moved forward over the open plain, all men hoped, and rejoiced in the assurance, that the object of the expedition was gained.   For already were the General's proclamations carried far and wide through the country.   The people were invited to continue in their dwellings.   They were warned against ill-using or carrying off the prisoners, and promised protection, if, by their behaviour, they should show themselves worthy of it, and both assurances were repeated as soon as the head-quarter tent was pitched on the race-course, within three English miles of the Balla Hissar of Cabul.

Though every precaution was taken to hinder the spread of a panic through the country, nobody was surprised to find that the impulse spread wider and wider as the army advanced.   Not a human being had been met in all the way from Bootkak to Cabul, and now that the camp was set up outside the city walls, the city was found to be deserted.   A few chiefs who either had been, or professed to have been friendly when the British army was in its difficulties, abode in their houses ; and of the lowest of the people a good many remained to take their chance ; but the bazaars were deserted, the shops emptied of their contents, and the owners both of shops and wares fled, no one could tell whither.   In like manner the Balla Hissar, abandoned by its garrison, stood with open gates to be dealt with as the stranger might determine.   It was immediately occupied by detachments from different infantry regiments, whose measured tread brought echoes from the vaulted passages; and who having hoisted on its loftiest pinnacle the standard of England, took possession of such apartments as seemed best suited to their own convenience.

For obvious reasons it was desirable to reopen the markets of Cabul; and while fresh proclamations invited the dealers to return, evidence was afforded of the general's determination to respect the rights of persons and of property, by the steadiness with which he restrained his men from entering the city. Guards were placed at the different gates, and neither soldier nor camp follower was permitted to go beyond them, unless he produced a written pass or order, signed by the general of the brigade or division to which he was attached. The result was that the natives began, ere long, to anticipate a renewal of the policy of a former year.   They began to come back, first by twos and threes, by and by a hundred or two at a time, and ultimately by thousands.   Accordingly, before the expiration of many days, the bazaars became what they used to be, the shops were filled with goods, and the streets were crowded with people; between whom and the inhabitants of the camp a traffic was established, which proved for a while equally advantageous to both parties.

Meanwhile Akbar had fled, carrying with him the larger number of his prisoners.   Some the abiders in Cabul refused to send in his train; and these consisting of fourteen persons, of whom two were ladies and ten children, were escorted into camp. It is impossible to describe the forlorn condition of these poor people—one the widowed mother of eight infants—or to do justice to the kindness and delicate consideration with which they were treated.   Nevertheless, the recovery of so many seemed but to aggravate the feelings of those who mourned over friends and relatives still in the hands of the murderer of Sir William Macnaghten.   Accordingly, intrigue and negotiation with large promises of money were set afloat in all quarters, and applied to every one who was supposed to be approachable, through such a medium; and in due time matters were put in such a train as held out good promise of perfect success in the end.

Akbar Khan had retreated with the wreck of his army towards the Hindoo Koosh. He was heard of at Bameean on the 16th and 17th; and on the 18th the glad tidings spread through the camp, that one of his followers, Salee Mohammed by name, had been won over to betray his post, and was actually moving towards Cabul with the whole of the British prisoners. Sir Robert Sale had been observed by his officers that day to be unusually excited and restless. He was continually riding from his own tent to that of the General, and towards evening came back from one of these little journeys with the air of a man whose heart is full of deep emotion. His officers, who shared the anxieties of their chief, gathered round him; and when told that at length Lady Sale was safe, and that she and his widowed daughter Mrs. Sturt, were on the way to rejoin him, there arose a shout, which the men of the regiment soon took up, and which extended, as well as a knowledge of the circumstance that drew it forth, to the gallant 35th. It was a night of much joy, not unmixed with anxiety, in the camp; for the brigade knew that a force was to march at daybreak to meet the procession, and all were eager to have the privilege of being added to it.

How Lady Sale and her companions in misfortune had been carried from place to place at the will of the captor; how they fared in their captivity, and with what exceeding firmness they bore up against the trials to which they were exposed, are tales too well and too often told to require that I should repeat them. In like manner the narrative of their providential escape, just as they were on the eve of being carried whither the foot of European never could have followed, is familiar to the English public. Salee Mohammed, a chief of the tribe of Hazarees, had begun his political career, on the arrival of Lord Keane's army at Cabul, by espousing the cause of Shah Shujah. This he abandoned as soon as the tide of fortune seemed to set against him; and thenceforth became, for a while, one of the most active of Akbar Khan's partisans. But incapable of withstanding the influence of money, he was again won over for the second time

N

at a very critical moment in the progress of events. Having raised a strong force of his clansmen, he marched in the train of Akbar; and so ingratiated himself into his good graces, that the care of the prisoners was committed to him. Salee Moham-med desired no more. He had received one bribe, and had the assurance of another, and he now lingered with his charge till Akbar, having struck his tents, was proceeding at the head of the main body of his army through the Bameean pass into Balk. Salee now struck his tents in like manner, but instead of following in the track of Akbar, he doubled back through the hills, and by a circuitous route made his way towards Urghun-dee. Thither, on the 19th, Sale had proceeded at the head of his own regiment, and a force of artillery. Even Sale, however, was but the follower of Sir R. Shakespear, who, with five hun-dred Kuzylebashes, had pushed on to meet the prisoners; and afford them additional protection. But why go on with such details ? On the 20th of September, leaving his camp at Urghun-dee, Sir Robert Sale proceeded as far as a place called Jubeaiz ; whence, from the summit of a little pass, the captives were first seen, wending their way, peaceably and with apparent confidence, down the face of an opposite slope. Who will undertake to describe the emotions of all that witnessed or took part in that strange scene? The thunder of artillery told that day, not of the work of death in progress, but of its opposite. Friends met friends from whom they had long been parted. The wife threw herself into the arms of her husband; the daughter leaned upon her father's neck and wept; while a royal salute, fired from the horse artillery that had come to the rescue, called echoes from the distant hills which seemed to laugh and shout with joy as they spake.

CHAPTER XXIII.

Evacuation of Afghanistan.

WHILE Sale with his gallant followers conducted back their liberated friends in triumph, an expedition was fitted out by the commander-in-chief at Cabul; and sent to disperse a band of rebels which had gathered under the banner of a Kohistan chief, and established itself at Istaliff. Of the extreme beauty of that place, and of the surrounding country, I took occasion to speak while describing the movements of the force which headed back Dost Mohammed from Purandurrah. Standing upon the side of a mountain, which is overhung with gardens and orchards in terraces, Istaliff, both for the salubrity of its climate and the exquisite loveliness of its scenery, is without a rival in Central Asia; and being surrounded by walls, with towers here and there, so planted as to be very difficult of approach, it offers to the soldier a military position of no ordinary strength. There a considerable body of Afghans had drawn together; and a holy war being by Akbar's directions proclaimed, they gave out, from day to day, that they should presently advance upon Cabul, destroy the unbelievers, and liberate the place. They were anticipated in this generous purpose by the march of General MacCaskill and a division of the army towards their stronghold. A smart affair ensued, which ended, as all such were accustomed to do, in the total defeat of the enemy; and the town being entered sword in hand, it was given up to plunder. No lives were, however, taken after resistance ceased. A large number of women and children were, indeed, secured, and placed under guard, only that they might be sent back, without ransom, as soon as the fighting ceased, to their friends; but they were treated throughout with marked tenderness, neither insult nor injury being offered to them. It cannot be said, however, that much mercy was shown to the property of the people. Istaliff was the capital of a district which had rendered itself conspicuous

N 2

during the troubles of 1841 for the cruel and treacherous conduct of its chiefs and people to their European visitors. Here
were cut off, while dwelling at peace in the midst of them,
Lieutenant Rattray and Captain Codrington, both in the Company's service ; and here, also, Major Pottinger sustained much
suffering, his followers being slain, and himself escaping, covered
with wounds, as if by a miracle. These things were not forgotten by the troops who forced an entrance that day into Istaliff; and it was this remembrance which urged them to the per-
petration of a work of vengeance, which must continue to be felt
as long as the present generation shall last: for they did not
leave a house standing. Fire consumed both castle and cottage ;
and gardens, vineyards, orchards, &c., were all cut down. Had
there been at hand sufficient means of transport, the victors
would have returned to Cabul encumbered with spoil. As it
was, they cast into the flames every article, no matter how costly,
which was too cumbersome to be conveyed about the persons of
the men.

Having thus re-established the prestige of British invincibility
(for General Nott had marched in triumph from the side of
Candahar, winning back Ghuznee, and overthrowing with great
slaughter every armed body which ventured to face him), General
Pollock made ready, in agreement with the orders under which
'he acted, to return to the British provinces. A son of Shah
Shujah, Futteh Jung by name, had hoisted his standard over
the Balla Hissar, and proclaimed himself king. Few men of any
note rallied under it; and the weak young man was given dis-
tinctly to understand that he need not look to the Feringhees for
the support which his own countrymen withheld from him. At
the same time the Balla Hissar was freely given up to him ; and
because he besought that it might be spared, the General neither
broke down the walls nor suffered a torch to be applied to the
wood-work. But every gun that was found in the place he
caused to be destroyed ; and blew up as many of his own batter-
ing-train as he found that he was without strength of cattle to
drag through the passes. Having settled these points, General
Pollock gave directions for inflicting upon the guilty capital the
punishment which it deserved. With natural vanity Akbar
Khan had built a mosque to commemorate the destruction of

Elphinstone's force, to which he gave the name of the Feringhee Mosque, and which his flatterers affected to regard as one of the wonders of the world. It was levelled with the ground; and then followed the blowing up of the bazaars, the burning of chiefs' houses, the destruction of the city gates, and, last of all, a conflagration which spread everywhere till the waters of the river stayed it. That the work of plunder could be wholly stopped, amid the confusion attendant on such proceedings, was not to be expected. In spite of guards, camp-followers and soldiers made their way into the burning town, and loaded themselves with articles, scarcely one of which they were able, after the march began, to carry beyond the encampment. And here and there accidents occurred, of which it speaks well in praise of the discipline of the force that they were not multiplied fifty-fold.

The work of destruction began upon the 7th of October. It continued all that day and the next, and throughout both nights; and, indeed, till the mountains of the Bootkak shut it from them, the soldiers of Sale's brigade saw the whole face of the sky red with the flames which they had contributed to raise. But Sale's brigade did not linger long near the ruins of the Afghan capital; for on the 12th of October the army began its march towards the provinces. It moved by divisions, the first, to which the garrison of Jellalabad was attached, leading. It threaded the passes, not altogether unopposed, yet without sustaining any serious inconvenience; and having abandoned and destroyed a few heavy guns, which, for lack of draft animals, could not be carried forward, came in, in due time, to Jellalabad. That city shared the fate of Cabul and Ghuznee: it was razed to the ground; and the sick being moved forward, and the detachments gathered in which had heretofore protected them and maintained posts of halt for the main body, the whole proceeded through the Khyber and the Punjaub to the Sutlej.

So ended a war begun for no wise purpose, carried on with a strange mixture of rashness and timidity, and brought to a close, after suffering and disaster, without much of glory attaching either to the government which directed, or the great body of the troops which waged it. One portion of the army of the Indus did, indeed, win for itself a fame which shall be deathless.

The garrison of Jellalabad well earned the epithet which the Governor-General, by his proclamation, bestowed upon it. But as soon as we avert our eyes from the heroic deeds of that handful of men, there is not much in the military history of those times on which we shall care to rest them. Doubtless, the massacre of the Koord Cabul was avenged. By the destruction of their chief towns, and the devastation of their villages and orchards, the Afghans were taught that England is powerful to punish as well as to protect. And in all the encounters with the armed men who resisted them, our soldiers proved themselves to be both dauntless and enduring. But not one benefit, either political or military, has England acquired by the war. Indeed, our evacuation of the country resembled almost as much the retreat of an army defeated as the march of a body of conquerors, seeing that to the last our flanks and rear were attacked, and that such baggage as we did save, we saved by dint of hard fighting. Nevertheless, the gates of Somnauth were carried back to the land whence Nadir had removed them; and British India proclaimed, what the whole world good-naturedly allowed, that we had redeemed our honour, and were once more victorious.

THE END.

www.ingramcontent.com/pod-product-compliance
Lightning Source LLC
Chambersburg PA
CBHW030403100426
42812CB00028B/2818/J